W9-ANA-595

Modern Critical Views

Modern Critical Views

Modern Critical Views

MATTHEW ARNOLD

Edited and with an introduction by

Harold Bloom
Sterling Professor of the Humanities
Yale University

CHELSEA HOUSE PUBLISHERS
New York ◇ Philadelphia

Library of Congress Cataloging-in-Publication Data
Matthew Arnold.
    (Modern critical views)
    Bibliography: p.
    Includes index.
    1. Arnold, Matthew, 1822–1888—Criticism and
interpretation. I. Bloom, Harold. II. Series.
PR4024.M373 1986   821'.8   86-17089
ISBN 0-87754-686-X

Contents

Editor's Note

This volume gathers together a representative selection of the best contemporary criticism devoted to the poetry and prose of Matthew Arnold, arranged here in the chronological order of its original publication. I am grateful to Hillary Kelleher for her assistance in editing this book.

My introduction centers on Arnold's conflict with himself, as a poet, a conflict in which his Romantic sensibility gradually yielded to a Classical critical ideal. W. H. Auden's poem on Arnold sees this conflict as an Oedipal struggle with Dr. Thomas Arnold and is reprinted here as an eloquent epigraph to the chronological sequence of criticism.

J. Hillis Miller, in his earlier phase as a "critic of consciousness," follows Auden in a vision of Arnold as a sage who rejects the present and embalms a dead wisdom. This vision is related to Geoffrey Tillotson's account of Arnold's theory and practice as a prose writer, since Tillotson concludes that Arnold's prime fault is that he tried to combine urbanity with posturing, both difficult stances in a seer who denounces all of present time.

A very sympathetic reading of "The Scholar-Gipsy" by G. Wilson Knight provides a gentler perspective upon Arnold's quest for wisdom than any we have yet been afforded. Equally sympathetic is the essay of William Robbins, who finds in some of Arnold's letters to Clough the seedbed of the cultural prophecy of subsequent years. The most sympathetic of these defenses of Arnold is by William E. Buckler, who traces in Arnold's Classical stance, as a critic, the prelude to T. S. Eliot's similar position.

Arnold's later phase, as a writer rationalizing religion, is the subject of Ruth apRoberts, who concludes that the Arnoldian ideal of culture subsumed religion as it subsumed all of literature. A. Dwight Culler, Arnold's most authoritative critic since Lionel Trilling, presents an overview of Arnold's cultural achievement as reflecting the main movement of mind in his age, with a gradual transition from an emphasis upon the Greek Classics to the late preoccupation with the Bible.

In this book's final essay, printed here for the first time, Sara Suleri analyzes Arnold's major poem *Empedocles on Etna* as a manifesto for the rise of a literary culture—replacing philosophy, religion, and science—by centering poetry upon the figure of the reader, a swerve into a new kind of poetic possibility, executed at the expense of many of the older possibilities. Suleri's subtle balance suggests that Arnold's conversion of his anxiety of belatedness into an academic pleasure of contemplation was at best a qualified success.

Introduction

Arnold is a Romantic poet who did not wish to be one, an impossible conflict which caused him finally to abandon poetry for literary criticism and prose prophecy. From the middle 1850s on, Arnold was primarily a prose writer, and his influence has been largely as a literary critic.

Arnold was born on December 24, 1822, the eldest son of the formidable Dr. Thomas Arnold, who from 1828 on was to be Headmaster of Rugby School. Dr. Arnold, a historian of some limited distinction, was a Protestant moralist of the rationalizing kind. His son did well at Rugby but alarmed Dr. Arnold with a defensive posture of continuous gaiety, which became a mock-dandyism at Balliol College, Oxford, where his closest friend was the poet Arthur Hugh Clough. After a fellowship at Oriel College, Oxford, Arnold went to London in 1847, as private secretary to a high official. In 1849 his early poems were published as *The Strayed Reveller, and Other Poems*. The "Marguerite" of those poems is now known to have been inspired by a youthful infatuation with Mary Claude, a summertime neighbor in the Lake district. In 1850, he fell in love with a judge's daughter, whom he married in 1851, after being appointed an Inspector of Schools.

In 1852 Arnold published his principal poem, the ambitious and uneasy *Empedocles on Etna*. When he brought together his *Poems* in 1853, he excluded *Empedocles*, explaining in the volume's famous anti-Romantic Preface that passive suffering was not a fit theme for poetry. When in 1857, he was elected Professor of Poetry at Oxford, almost all his best poetry had been written. Thus, his next poem, *Merope. A Tragedy*, published in 1858, is rather frigid, and the outstanding poems of his last volume, *New Poems* (1867), were composed many years before.

Whatever his achievement as a critic of literature, society, or religion, his work as a poet may not merit the reputation it has continued to hold in the twentieth century. Arnold is, at his best, a very good but highly derivative poet, unlike Tennyson, Browning, Hopkins, Swinburne, and Rossetti, all of whom individualized their voices. As with Tennyson, Hopkins, and Rossetti, Arnold's dominant precursor was Keats, but this is an unhappy puzzle, since Arnold (unlike the others) professed not to admire Keats greatly, while writing his own elegiac poems in a diction, meter, imagistic procedure, that are embarrassingly close to Keats (any reader who believes that this judgment is too harsh ought to experiment immediately by reading side-by-side the odes of Keats and Arnold's "The Scholar-Gipsy" or "Thyrsis"). Tennyson, Hopkins, and D. G. Rossetti retain distinctive Keatsian elements in their mature styles, but these elements are subdued to larger effects. But Arnold in "The Scholar-Gipsy," his best poem of some length, uses the language and movement of Keats even though the effect is irrelevant to his poem's theme.

Still, it is not a mean distinction to have written lyrics as strong as the famous "To Marguerite—Continued" and "Dover Beach" or a meditative poem as profound as "The Buried Life." Arnold got into his poetry what Tennyson and Browning scarcely needed (but absorbed anyway), the main march of mind in his time. His frequently dry tone and flatness of statement may not have been, as he happily believed, evidences of Classicism, but of a lack of poetic exuberance, a failure in the vitality of his language. But much abides in his work, and he is usefully prophetic also of the anti-Romantic "Modernism" of our time, so much of which, like Arnold, has turned out to be Romantic in spite of itself.

W. H. AUDEN

"Matthew Arnold"

His gift knew what he was—a dark disordered city;
Doubt hid it from the father's fond chastising sky;
Where once the mother-farms had glowed protectively,
Stood the haphazard alleys of the neighbours' pity.

—Yet would have gladly lived in him and learned his ways,
And grown observant like a beggar, and become
Familiar with each square and boulevard and slum,
And found in the disorder a whole world to praise.

But all his homeless reverence, revolted, cried:
"I am my father's forum and he shall be heard,
Nothing shall contradict his holy final word,
Nothing." And thrust his gift in prison till it died,

And left him nothing but a jailor's voice and face,
And all rang hollow but the clear denunciation
Of a gregarious optimistic generation
That saw itself already in a father's place.

From *Another Time: Poems.* © 1940 and renewed 1968 by W. H. Auden. Random House, 1940.

J. HILLIS MILLER

Matthew Arnold

How can the kingdom of God be brought back to earth? Man now is "naked, eternally restless mind." The joy of immediacy is his no longer. He must therefore seek something which will *mediate* between him and his lost home. Arnold's early poetry and his letters to Clough are the record of his search for some means to escape from the intolerable situation of detachment and aimless drifting. This testing of various forms of mediation continued all his life.

In the epoch of harmony there were no time and space in the usual sense, for the temporal and spatial dimensions of things bound them together rather than separating them, as all times and spaces are equally present to God. The disintegration which produced our world divided everything into fragments, with man isolated in the middle, able to turn toward each one separately, but never able to possess them all at once. It may be that the "world's multitudinousness" is a prismatic diffraction of the original unity rather than a complete dispersal of broken pieces. Certainly Arnold rejects the division of *man's* nature into multiple faculties. Against this modern psychological theory he sets his notion that each man is inwardly and secretly one, as coral islands, separate on the surface, are joined in the deeps. If the world external to man is also a unity hidden behind apparent diversity then it would be possible to reach that unity by following any one of the separate elements far enough, with self-forgetful intensity. Only by experimentation could the poet discover which of the two grand alternatives is correct,

From *The Disappearance of God: Five Nineteenth-Century Writers.* © 1963 by the President and Fellows of Harvard College. The Belknap Press of Harvard University Press, 1963.

whether the broken pieces of the world are discontinuous with their origin, or whether the world, though multiple, is still connected, by however remote a series of gradations, with its source.

Just these alternatives and their consequences are balanced against one another in an important poem called "In Utrumque Paratus." Arnold at this time (the poem was first published in 1849) cannot commit himself to either possibility, but declares himself "ready for either." The two alternatives would lead to radically different conceptions of the human condition. If the present world of multiplicity is the result of a gradual "procession," a spherical expansion in all directions from an original and central "One all-pure," then, however far we have come from the moment of the primal birth of things, it would still be possible to "remount" the "colour'd dream / Of life" and reach, beyond all diverse colors, the white source of all. This remounting would mean isolation from the present fragmented times, but it would be an isolation and purity reached through these fragments, not by a discontinuous leap beyond them, for they still participate in their secret source, and are a means of reaching it.

On the other hand, it is possible that the multitudinous world has no divine origin or else has completely broken with that origin. If this is so, then the world must be defined materialistically, as the aimless combination and recombination of elements which have existed as an isolated brute mass from all time. The world is a "wild unfather'd mass," and has had "no birth / In divine seats." If such is the situation, then no retrogressive remounting of the stream of life will ever reach anything essentially different from the present condition of things.

There is no way to tell which theory is correct, no way but by testing the various strands of this diversely colored life to see if any of them leads back to the One. Like the hero of Browning's "Numpholeptos," Arnold must try first the red ray, then the green, and so on until the whole rainbow has been exhausted. Whereas Browning's nympholept goes out toward the periphery, Arnold must try to reach directly the white light at the center which is the source of all color.

The most obvious reference of the image of "life's stream" in "In Utrumque Paratus" is to time. The image of time as a stream flowing from the high mountains of the past toward the distant sea of the future is one of the basic configurations of Arnold's imagination, appearing recurrently in his poetry, and, more covertly, in his prose, as in the famous definition of God as the "stream of tendency by which all things strive to fulfill the law of their being." The image of the river of time pictures man's early history as taking place in the uplands or mountains near the source of the river, where the air is clear and pure. Now, in these latter days, we are flowing through the hot, flat plain, where the river is bordered by crowded cities, and our lives are determined by this heat and confusion, "changing and shot as the sights which we see."

As Maurice Merleau-Ponty has shown, the spatial representation of time as a river is full of ambiguities, however natural it may be to think of time in this way. Time is not the flowing river; it is a *relation* between the river and someone watching it. But the image changes bewilderingly depending on where we put the observer. If one imagines oneself standing on the bank watching time flow by, the past is not upstream, but downstream, where lie the waters which have already passed by. The ocean into which the river flows is not the mysterious future, but is the dumping ground of the past. The future lies upstream, where the waters are flowing which have not yet reached us. Only if we imagine ourselves as flowing with the river, as Arnold does in "The Future" and elsewhere, is the past upstream and the future downstream. In this case the river does not possess the contents of time. These already exist along the banks, in a spatial row, waiting to be passed by a point on the moving river. The river does not have any content, only the perpetual present of its motion past things. We do not move in relation to the river at all, but are a fixed point on an endless belt. Time is not a dimension of things. They remain fixed eternally on the banks. Only the river moves, the river and the empty mind of man which is identified with a point on it. If we think of the river of time simultaneously from the points of view of the river and of the bank, as we are inclined to do, and as Arnold often does, then the ambiguity is complete. We are thinking of time at once as our motion past things, and as the motion of things past us. Time is both something moving and something still which we we move past. In the same way past and future coincide in whichever direction we look, upstream or downstream. The image of time as a river, when examined, reveals itself as absurd and contradictory, but it is a rich absurdity, and a suggestive contradiction, as is proved by the many uses of the image, from Heraclitus' famous river, and the Platonic image of time as a moving image of eternity, to Yeats's river of time in "The Old Men Admiring Themselves in the Water" or "The Needle's Eye," and Eliot's use of the Mississippi in the "Four Quartets."

Though there is no evidence that Arnold was aware of the ambiguities of his image of time he manipulates them strategically, as in his constant suggestion that the origin and ending of time are the same. All man has lost by moving away from the "sources of time" he will recover when at last he reaches the sea. In "The Buried Life," one of Arnold's most important

explorations of the image of the river, the poet affirms that to possess for a
moment the "unregarded river of our life" is to possess simultaneously "The
hills where [our] life rose, / And the sea where it goes." If the ending turns
back on the beginning time is a circle, and every moment of time, though
it seems isolated from the origin and end of time, is as close to God as the
very first moment of creation. As in the old Plotinian or Augustinian theory
of time, each moment, though part of an endless succession, partakes of the
motionless plenitude of God:

> Thus yesterday, to-day, to-morrow come,
> They hustle one another and they pass;
> But all our hustling morrows only make
> The smooth to-day of God.

Just as Arnold identifies beginning and ending, upstream and downstream on the river of time, so his use of the image also suggests that man
is simultaneously flowing with the river and living in the bristling cities on
the plain. If he is the isolated mind which runs with time and sees each
object on the bank for only a moment, he is also the contents of the mind,
and dwells, however fleetingly, in fixed abodes on the bank. Arnold's sense
of his simultaneous detachment from life and enforced participation in it is
perfectly expressed in the ambiguous relations between flowing water and
fixed bank in the image of the river of time.

Does time, conceived of according to this image, permit any escape from
the intolerable present? Though the image suggests the irresistible compul-
sion of time driving man from one moment to another, nevertheless, if time
is a river, each moment is bound to the others in a succession so unbroken
as to form a fluid continuity. If this is the case man might be able to "remount"
the stream of time and reach the primal unity. Remount in what fashion?
Arnold has been momentarily misled by his image. Time is not, like space,
a fixed expanse which can be traversed in any direction by motion through
it. Time is a one-way flow, and the moments which belong to the past can
never be recaptured as present again. Arnold is truer to his experience of
time when he describes his limitation to just the moment of time he is
experiencing now, and even more true when he laments his inability even
to hold on to the present. Time flows on remorselessly and tears him away
from moments of pleasure or satisfied desire.

The most poignant versions of this theme have to do with Arnold's
sense that the failure of love in these bad times is caused by the implacable
flow of time. Time bears the lovers apart. "A Dream," for example, uses
the image of the river of time to express the nightmare of an inability to

reach the loved one. Though she beckons invitingly with her companion from the shore, "the river of Life, / Loud thundering, [bears him] by."

Is there no power by which he may repossess the past? For other poets, for Arnold's much-admired Wordsworth, memory is the faculty which recaptures the past. What is Arnold's experience of memory?

His earliest poem about memory is the first of the Marguerite poems, "A Memory-Picture." Here, tormented by his premonition that the present happy hour with Marguerite will pass, he forces himself to fix the moment on his memory so that he may keep it always. If "Time's current strong / Leaves us fixt to nothing long," perhaps we can cheat time by preserving the past indelibly in memory. Though the memory-picture is only a "dim remembrance" of actuality, it is something at least preserved from time's obliterating power, and so the poet cries, "Quick, thy tablets, Memory!"

The note of urgency in these lines betrays Arnold's lack of faith in the power of memory. He has no experience of involuntary affective memory, the Proustian or Wordsworthian reminiscence which brings back the past in all its freshness of sensible immediacy; he also lacks the power of a willed and rational memory, the memory which seizes violently on the present moment and forces it to abide. Rather than enjoying the involuntary rising up of "spots of time" from the depths of the past, Arnold must suffer the involuntary disappearance of whatever once belonged to him, but now belongs only to an unapproachable past: "And we forget because we must / And not because we will."

In one poem Arnold is tormented by his knowledge that though the past cannot be recaptured in memory, nevertheless he will be able to remember that there is something which he cannot remember. If the "stedfast commandment of Nature / Wills that remembrance should always decay," if mere absence from the loved one means the gradual disappearance of her image from his heart, Arnold would prefer to forget Marguerite completely, as soon as he leaves her, so that if he were to meet her again she would appear as a stranger. Since total memory is impossible Arnold asks for a total forgetting: "Me let no half-effaced memories cumber! / . . . Dead be the past and its phantoms to me!"

Arnold is able neither to forget nor to remember. He is condemned to be visited by half-effaced memories of events he can neither escape nor repossess. The Marguerite poems are the expression of this ambiguous relation to the past, a relation which offers no means of remounting the stream of life and reaching the "One."

The past is no pathway to the lost harmony, and its exploration only confirms Arnold in his isolation. What of the future? Since beginning and ending coincide in Arnold's theory of time, he might be able to reach what he has lost in the past by moving forward into the future.

Arnold finds a way to console himself for the way he is torn from pleasures as soon as he gets them, or is unable to reach them at all. Though it seems that he is eddying about in blind uncertainty, he is guided secretly by the unregarded river of his life. This "buried stream" is the inalienable law of his being, a law which is at once within him and outside him. It makes him break allegiances for which he is not destined, and drives him on toward a hidden goal. When he reaches this goal he will recover his "genuine self," and at the same time regain the intimacy with all things he has lost since the green sources of time. Man is forced by an "unknown Power" to move on unceasingly with time, but since his life has a hidden direction and end, it is perhaps truer to say that he is drawn from the future by this goal than that he is driven by the past: "For this and that way swings / The flux of mortal things, / Though moving inly to one far-set goal."

This view of time permits Arnold to assuage his sense of guilt for his unconquerable coldness and want of spontaneous feeling. It takes away his anguished feeling that it is *his* fault his love affair with Marguerite has been a failure. He cannot help it if he is "three parts iced over." If the far-set goal is drawing him ceaselessly on, he is not responsible for being unable to love Marguerite as he wishes. It is the unknown God who drives him away from a love which is not destined to be his. It is possible to say that Arnold was hiding from himself his responsibility for his fiasco with Marguerite, but the motif appears often enough to show that it gave Arnold plausible solace:

> Who renders vain their deep desire?—
> A God, a God their severance ruled!
> And bade betwixt their shores to be
> The unplumb'd, salt, estranging sea.
>
> Again I spring to make my choice;
> Again in tones of ire
> I hear a God's tremendous voice:
> "Be counsell'd, and retire."

In spite of the consolations of this idea, to believe that he is secretly moving toward a reconciliation with all he has lost does not change Arnold's experience of the present. It remains a directionless eddying, a "tedious tossing to and fro," a wandering in the desert. In "Rugby Chapel," one of Arnold's most hopeful poems about the future, the poet opposes the "eddy of purposeless dust" of most men's lives to the sense of a clearly seen goal

possessed by his father and others like him. As the poem proceeds it becomes
clear that the goal is only an object of implicit faith. The actual present is
a wandering in a rocky wasteland with no sight of the "bound of the waste":

> A God
> Marshall'd them, gave them their goal.
> Ah, but the way is so long!
>
> . . . .
>
>   Sole they shall stray; in the rocks
> Stagger for ever in vain,
> Die one by one in the waste.

Arnold best expresses his experience of time in a much earlier poem,
"Resignation." That poem begins by saying that all men need to propose to
themselves a goal which they may reach before death and which, "gain'd,
may give repose." Our life does not fulfill this need. Arnold's temporal
experience is here expressed in the description of a band of gypsies who, far
from proceeding toward a goal, wander homelessly from one place to another,
often returning by accident to a place where once before they had pitched
their tents. Time is not a progression at all, but a meaningless repetition, a
repetition from moment to moment as long as life lasts of the same sense of
deracination and infinite distance from the promised land. Whether Arnold
looks toward the past or toward the future, time offers him no way out of
the present sequence of moments each repeating the same suffering and
isolation.

If not time, then what of space, or the contents of space, the physical
things which surround us in the present moment? If the image of the river
of time is a misattribution of the traversability of space to the realm of time,
will space offer that access to the center of reconciliation which time forbids?
It can be crossed in any direction, and what dwells in space, nature, has
often been seen as the earthly abiding place of an immanent spiritual force
which is absent from man and his cities.

Arnold fluctuates in his doctrine of nature. Under the influence of the
romantic poets, he tries to experience nature in the Wordsworthian way,
and to feel that if he could only get outside himself he would find in nature
a source of perennial vitality. In "The Youth of Nature" he praises Wordsworth for being "a priest to us all / Of the wonder and bloom of the world,
/ Which we saw with his eyes, and were glad," and in his essay on Maurice
de Guérin he defines the power of poetry as the ability to give us an intimate
communication with nature and with the secret which nature contains: "The
grand power of poetry is its interpretative power; by which I mean, not a

power of drawing out in black and white an explanation of the mystery of the universe, but the power of so dealing with things as to awaken in us a wonderfully full, new, and intimate sense of them, and of our relations with them. When this sense is awakened in us, as to objects without us, we feel ourselves to be in contact with the essential nature of those objects, to be no longer bewildered and oppressed by them, but to have their secret, and to be in harmony with them; and this feeling calms and satisfies us as no other can." In "Lines Written in Kensington Gardens" Arnold speaks of the ever-new peace of nature, a peace which is a participation in the central One, the "calm soul of all things," and he prays to share in this peace. Arnold envies nature's ability to act without feverish anxiety and hurry, her "toil unsever'd from tranquillity."

Is it so certain that the peace of nature comes from a sharing in the divine life? It may be that nature is calm because isolation from God does not cause her to suffer as man does. Arnold sometimes reads in nature a lesson of grim endurance, the endurance of being just this bit of rock or turf here, untransfigured by any spiritual presence:

> the mute turf we tread,
> The solemn hills around us spread,
> This stream which falls incessantly,
> The strange-scrawl'd rocks, the lonely sky,
> If I might lend their life a voice,
> Seem to bear rather than rejoice.

Nature was once part of the divine order, and the stars were true sons of Heaven, imbued with a spiritual vitality, and possessors of a radiant joy. They "moved joyfully / Among august companions, / In an older world, peopled by Gods." Now the stars, like man, are cut off from the divine joy, shine coldly with their own lonely light, and move in their courses by blind necessity. They are "unwilling lingerers" in the wilderness of space, strangers both to heaven and to man, "without friend and without home."

Such natural things are superior to man only in that they have been able to endure isolation from God without suffering. Nature, unlike man, has kept some remnants of "an immortal vigour" in its heart, and has "in solitude / Maintain'd courage and force." But nature has this "free, light, cheerful air" only because it has utterly forgotten its divine origin. Man is closer to God than nature is just because man knows of his distance from God and suffers because of it. Arnold, in this mood, denies to the empty heavens any least memory of their suffering when they were separated from

God: "I will not say that your mild deeps retain / A tinge, it may be, of their silent pain / Who have long'd deeply once, and long'd in vain." The heavens have the calm and freedom of a corpse from which the spirit has fled, but it is better to be "untroubled and unpassionate" than to suffer, as Arnoldian man must suffer, the continual torments of being separated from one's true self and knowing it.

In such passages Arnold proposes a very different picture of nature from Wordsworth's. Far from being, though apparently divided, actually one, a deep harmony in which man and nature share together in the inalienable presence of "something far more deeply interfused," Arnold's world has split apart. Nature is separated from man, and is a collection of unrelated fragments juxtaposed without order or form. Each rock, bird, tree, or cloud is self-enclosed and separate from all the others.

Arnold's inability to see nature in the romantic way is constantly betrayed by the landscapes in his poetry. All the complexity of romantic nature poetry is, for the most part, missing in Arnold, and his poetry is by comparison thin and two-dimensional. This flatness is of great significance, and reveals a new phase in the spiritual history of Western man. Not at all times can poets see in the meanest flower that blows a mysterious expression of the whole universe.

Arnold has no sense of a harmonizing power in nature, nor can he express the Coleridgean sense that each object, though unique, is at the same time a symbol of the totality. Each object means itself, and is not a symbol of anything further. Landscapes in his poetry are often a neutral backdrop before which the action takes place. The closest Arnold can come to the multi-dimensional symbolism of romantic poetry is the simple equation of allegory, in which some human meaning or value is attached from the outside to a natural object. This produces locutions in which a concrete thing and an abstraction are yoked by violence together, as in the "sea of life," the "Sea of Faith," the "vasty hall of death," the "icebergs of the past," and so on. Try as he will Arnold cannot often get depth and resonance in his landscapes, and his descriptive passages tend to become unorganized lists of natural objects. The disorder and flatness of these lists betray Arnold's sense that nature is just a collection of discrete things, all jumbled up together, with no pattern or hierarchy. Arnold's nature, like his own life, is repetitive, the repetition of more examples of the same objects, or of more views of the same disorder. In "Resignation," he describes his return with his sister to a scene he has visited ten years before. "Here sit we," he says, "and again unroll, / Though slowly, the familiar whole." The scene is not really, it

turns out, a "whole." There is no transfiguration of a revisited scene, as in
"Tintern Abbey," and the suggestions of continuity in "unroll" are not
supported by what follows:

> The solemn wastes of heathy hill
> Sleep in the July sunshine still;
> The self-same shadows now, as then,
> Play through this grassy upland glen;
> The loose dark stones on the green way
> Lie strewn, it seems, where then they lay;
> On this mild bank above the stream,
> (You crush them!) the blue gentians gleam.
> Still this wild brook, the rushes cool,
> The sailing foam, the shining pool!

Hill, shadows, gentians; brook, rushes, foam, pool—the scene is a collection
of the elements which happen by accident to be there, "strewn" about like
the haphazard stones which lie in the center of the picture. There is no
grouping, no inner force molding all to a unity, no "instress" such as Hopkins
finds in nature, no interior tendency toward pattern or form. Everything is
slack. The scene, if it expresses anything, expresses the disintegration of
nature. When Arnold tries to be most like the romantic poets, as in the
pastiche of Keats in "The Scholar-Gipsy," he is really least like them, in
spite of his attempt to show the "interinanimation" of natural things. The
esemplastic force sweeping through nature in the romantic vision has fled
away and left dry isolated husks behind. In Arnold's hands nature poetry
becomes like descriptions in a botanical handbook—accurate, but superficial:

> Through the thick corn the scarlet poppies peep,
> And round green roots and yellowing stalks I see
> Pale pink convolvulus in tendrils creep;
> And air-swept lindens yield
> Their scent, and rustle down their perfumed showers
> Of bloom on the bent grass where I am laid.

If nature is just a collection of things, it is hopeless to seek any spiritual
presence there which might be a support for man. Imitating nature or seeking
harmony with nature no longer means trying to plunge our roots, like nature's, in the ground of the absolute, or trying, through atunement with
nature, to reach that ground. Each man must imitate nature in her mute
acceptance of separation from God, and be like a stone, rounded in upon
himself, with a stone's independence and persistence in being itself. Joy

comes not from participation in the general life, but from a blind perseverance in performing the acts appropriate to our own natures. The stars and the sea are "Bounded by themselves, and unregardful / In what state God's other works may be," and they "demand not that the things without them / Yield them love, amusement, sympathy." Yet they perform their appointed tasks with joy. Each man must also learn to be a law unto himself: "To its own impulse every creature stirs; / Live by thy light, and earth will live by hers!"

This lesson of nature is really a lesson of despair, for though nature is to be admired for her ability to endure isolation, this calm self-enclosure, the satisfied peace of a rock merely being a rock, is impossible for man. Man's trouble is that he finds in himself no given law to direct his being. He desperately needs help from outside, someone or something to tell him what to do and who to be. Can nature do no more than bid man attempt something impossible?

Sometimes Arnold proposes a third doctrine of nature. In this third theory nature does possess a secret life which is also the divine life. The trouble is that this life can only be reached with great difficulty, if at all. The fullest statement of this theory is in a poem which, like so many of Arnold's poems about nature, is an explicit consideration of the Wordsworthian doctrine of the Nature Spirit. "The Youth of Nature" is apparently another lament for the death of the great poet who could see into the heart of nature and communicate what he saw there. But as the poem progresses it gradually changes its tone and modulates into a questioning of Wordsworth's power to read the secret of nature. Though the divine pulse beats at Nature's heart, there is no Wordsworthian filial bond through which that blood can flow also through *our* hearts. The "loveliness, magic, and grace" which Wordsworth saw in nature and expressed in his poetry were no illusion, no projection into nature of an idea of the mind, but even Wordsworth caught no more than an evanescent glimpse of them. Nature is the dwelling place of the divine spirit, but, as Nature tells the poet, man cannot reach and possess that spirit. There is also an ominous sentence in the essay on Maurice de Guérin, a sentence following the description of the power of poetry to give us the sense that we have nature's secret: "I will not now inquire whether this sense is illusive, whether it can be proved not to be illusive, whether it does absolutely make us possess the real nature of things." He will not ask, but in saying so he *does* ask, and radically puts in question the doctrine of poetry which he has just proposed. Nature possesses a hidden life, Arnold suggests, but poetry does not make us sharers in that life.

Accordingly, alongside the landscapes of mute objects, there is in Arnold's poetry another kind of landscape. This landscape expresses perfectly the notion that nature is the hiding place of an inner life which can only be guessed at or glimpsed momentarily. This new kind of landscape represents neither a nature which is the dwelling place of an immanent spirit, nor a nature which is disintegrated and dead. God is present, but present as something fleeting and ungraspable, something which remains tantalizingly just beyond our ken. Arnold often presents a moonlight or twilight scene, a scene with no definite barrier to our sight. The diffused light seems to offer a principle of continuity which puts the spectator in touch with the most distant spot he can see. Space can be crossed, and even without crossing it man can see, hear, or smell things which he cannot touch or hold. Space is a conducting medium. But this space, which seems to offer all that time withholds, does not really give man access to the divine ground of things. Though space can be traversed by sight, seeing does not reach any goal, however far it goes. Space in these nocturnal scenes gradually fades away toward a horizon of obscurity which is not itself an end, but a penetrable distance which is proof that there is, beyond any place eyesight can reach, more space, and beyond that more space again. Space can be crossed, but this crossing does not reach anything different from the spot where the spectator stands:

> In the deserted, moon-blanch'd street,
> How lonely rings the echo of my feet!
>
> . . . .
>   —but see!
> A break between the housetops shows
> The moon! and, lost behind her, fading dim
> Into the dewy dark obscurity
> Down at the far horizon's rim,
> Doth a whole tract of heaven disclose!
>
> Coldly, sadly descends
> The autumn-evening. The field
> Strewn with its dank yellow drifts
> Of wither'd leaves, and the elms,
> Fade into dimness apace,
> Silent.
>
> The sandy spits, the shore-lock'd lakes,
>   Melt into open, moonlit sea.
>
> They stand and listen; they hear
> The children's shouts, and at times,
> Faintly, the bark of a dog

From a distant farm in the hills.
Nothing besides! in front
The wide, wide valley outspreads
To the dim horizon, reposed
In the twilight, and bathed in dew,
Corn-field and hamlet and copse
Darkening fast.

"Fading dim," "fade into dimness," "melt into," "outspreads to the dim horizon," "darkening fast"—these are the characteristic motifs of this third kind of landscape, and with them goes a constant sense of the precariousness of the moment of insight. Only by twilight or moonlight, when space is filled with a soft light, can man's senses move well enough through space to discover that this movement only takes him out into a dim obscurity or into the manifest barrenness of "a whole tract of heaven" or the "open, moonlit sea." The moment of twilight is only a moment, and just as space itself fades into obscurity or emptiness, so the moment when we can have this knowledge is ephemeral, and is fast darkening toward night, when space will no longer betray its nature to the spectator. It is as if the impenetrable obscurity into which space fades were closing in on the beholder, absorbing the clearer space around him in its blackness.

The central essence of nature is not blackness. The center is the all-inclusive One from which issued the multiplicity of the world. This center is everywhere in nature, and yet is revealed only evanescently. It is something which evades direct perception, and retreats beyond the farthest limit our senses can reach. Arnold most reminds us of Tennyson when he apprehends nature as full of melancholy, broken, fugitive things, things which are the covert revelation of a deity who remains a presence-absence, hidden as much as made manifest in things, never quite tangibly there, but glimpsed in the very moment of disappearing:

Like bright waves that fall
With a lifelike motion
On the lifeless margin of the sparkling Ocean;
A wild rose climbing up a mouldering wall—
A gush of sunbeams through a ruin'd hall—
Strains of glad music at a funeral.

The waves, the rose, the sunbeams, and the music are images of something which has just emerged from occultation, and is about to return to its concealment.

Perhaps it is possible to pierce beyond these tantalizing appearances and reach what they momentarily reveal. In "Parting" Arnold rejects the lure of Marguerite, and chooses to follow the storm-winds of autumn which blow toward the mountains. If he can follow the winds he will reach the heart of nature. At that heart is the systole and diastole of forces, the expansion and contraction of the mists, which is the ever-repeated, ever-renewed process whereby space and time are born of what is beyond space and time, in "the stir of the forces / Whence issued the world."

Though Arnold makes his choice for movement up the mountains toward the center of things, he remains static. The pulls in opposite directions, up and down, toward the mountains and toward Marguerite (who comes *down* the stairs), balance, and the poet remains fixed in an immobile equilibrium. In no one of Arnold's poems about space is any real movement made. Though these poems establish an orientation in terms of up and down which is the spatial version of the river of time, there is in them all an atmosphere of poise. It is not possible to make true progress through Arnoldian space, for whatever new place is reached is transformed into another version of the old places. Nor is it possible to embrace the totality of space by the addition of local spaces. Man is driven by a frenzied desire to know all and possess all at once: "Look, the world tempts our eye, / And we would know it all!" But each man is limited to the spot where he is, and when he moves to a new place he loses possession of the place he has just left. As he progresses in his anxious attempt to reach totality by the addition of finite experiences he has a nightmarish sense that the sun of unexperienced things is growing larger rather than smaller: "But still, as we proceed / The mass swells more and more." Finally he must recognize the sad truth. Only God can know all the world at once. Man is limited to his own narrow perspective, and "Man's measures cannot mete the immeasurable All." Though each man's state of mind seems all-important to him, it does not extend beyond his own being. When he is happy, and would have the moment stay, there are ten thousand other human beings who are in misery, and would have the moment pass. Neither thought nor passion, however intense, can push out the barriers which limit each man to one little area of space:

> there's no mood,
> No meditation, no delight, no sorrow,
> Cas'd in one man's dimensions, can distil
> Such pregnant and infectious quality,
> Six yards round shall not ring it.—

Arnold's exploration of space has been no more successful than his exploration of time. Though man can move through space freely, both actually and with his senses, as he cannot move in time, it is impossible, however far he goes, to approach one inch closer to the secret of nature. Arnold's deepest experience of space is an anguished sense that he reaches, through space, all he most desires, but that this communication is a brief echo of something which remains infinitely distant, voices heard faintly and fleetingly across great spaces, "like wanderers from the world's extremity." A scarcely perceptible sound, a "strain, / From a far lonelier distance, like the wind," is man's only direct knowledge that something other than his present condition exists, but this dim knowledge is enough to make him homesick and melancholy, dissatisfied with his lot:

> Yet still, from time to time, vague and forlorn,
>
> . . . .
>
> As from an infinitely distant land,
> Come airs, and floating echoes, and convey
> A melancholy into all our day.

Neither space nor time offer a mediator between Arnoldian man and what he seeks. His testing of these two fundamental dimensions of his existence has served only to confirm more hopelessly his isolation.

Man is not only a creature of time and space, like a stone or a tree. He is also a social being, and can form relations to his fellows. Perhaps he can find in society or in the love of another person what he cannot find in time or space. In the lost epoch of harmony, love was still possible, and society was divinely ordered. This lost harmony would be regained if we could reestablish love or discover a valid society.

Only a still genuine society could be depended on to mediate between man and God. Present society does not appear to be so when seen from the point of view of isolated, self-conscious man, though this may be an illusion. The only way to make certain would be to accept the role society would have us play. There is in Arnold's writings a recurrent suspicion that the fault is not with the times, but with himself. His coldness and detachment may be preventing him from discovering whether any of the ways of living offered to him are valid ones.

Arnold is attracted by his own version of the strategy of role-playing. At present he is "an aimless unallay'd Desire." If he could act for a while as if one of the given ways of being were proper, he might find that the costume would become habitual dress. Arnold's copying in his notebooks of quotations of a courageous and morally stiffening sort was in one of its aspects an attempt to carry into practice this theory of role-playing. If he could go often enough through the act of writing down a solemn and con-structive quotation from some wise man of the past, Bishop Wilson or Isaiah or Epictetus, he might come to believe in the quotation and be made over in its image. Then "the best that has been thought and said in the world" would be made current in Arnold's own life.

This method of role-playing never really works for Arnold, in spite of the bulk of his notebooks. He is never able to conquer his coldness. Arnold makes a bad actor, and his own anxious face is always present behind the mask of Bishop Wilson, Sophocles, or Spinoza. Arnold is never able to leap beyond the basic paradox of such a strategy. There is no way to be certain that a given course of imitative action will lead to its goal. But how, unless we are sure, can we give ourselves wholeheartedly to any path? There is an element of guesswork in any choice of a predetermined way toward an end. If we were certain the path would lead to the goal, we should already in some sense possess the goal, and should not need to go through any process to reach it. It is just this unpredictability which Arnold is unwilling to accept. He has to see the goal clearly before he takes the plunge. My "one natural craving," he says, is "a distinct seeing of my way as far as my own nature is concerned." This is impossible. The goal stays hidden until it is reached. So Arnold remains permanently in his detachment, unable to accept any externally given code as the law of his being. At the crucial moment faith fails him, he throws down in disgust the mask of "duty self-denial etc.," and relaxes back into his usual inner slackness and anarchy: "What I must tell you," he writes to Clough, "is that I have never yet succeeded in any one great occasion in consciously mastering myself: I can go thro: the imaginary process of mastering myself and see the whole affair as it would then stand, but at the critical point I am too apt to hoist up the mainsail to the wind and let her drive. However as I get more awake to this it will I hope mend for I find that with me a clear almost palpable intuition (damn the logical sense of the word) is necessary before I get into prayer: unlike many people who set to work at their duty self-denial etc. like furies in the dark hoping to be gradually illuminated as they persist in this course."

The key word here is "intuition," and the strain Arnold is putting on the word is revealed in his exclamation about it. He recognizes that he wants the word to express a contradiction: the possession of the goal before one has gone through the process necessary to reach it. The "intuition" of the goal which Arnold requires before he starts praying must not be a vague supposition. It must be "clear" and "almost palpable," or else he cannot be sure enough that the goal is there to get under way at all. The peculiarity of prayer, from the human point of view, is that it creates in its own act the goal which is sought. Prayer brings us into the realm where prayer is answered. The other acts which Arnold is considering here are of the same nature. The strategy of escaping inner emptiness by the playing of a role must accept the initial obscurity and uncertainty of the method, but Arnold is unwilling to work like a fury in the dark hoping for a gradual illumination. So he remains withdrawn from life, the disinterested critic of the institutions, the literature, the society, the religion of his time. These present themselves to him never as something he has experienced from the inside, but as a spectacle to be regarded from a distance with a settled suspicion that the truth is not in them. As a critic of society he seeks rather to understand than to sympathize. He wants to control society and to keep it at arm's length by a discovery of its laws. His attitude toward society is fundamentally defensive. The "demand for an intellectual deliverance," he writes, "arises, because the present age exhibits to the individual man who contemplates it the spectacle of a vast multitude of facts awaiting and inviting his comprehension. The deliverance consists in man's comprehension of this present and past. It begins when our mind begins to enter into possession of the general ideas which are the law of this vast multitude of facts. It is perfect when we have acquired that harmonious acquiescence of mind which we feel in contemplating a grand spectacle that is intelligible to us."

Arnold strives to understand the spectacle of life by looking at it with the scientist's cold, detached eye, by "see[ing] the object as in itself it really is." Another name for this disinterestedness is irony, the stylistic pose which separates itself from what it describes, and, holding it at a distance, hollows it out with subtle mockery. Arnold is a skillful ironist, but his irony is not, as with the greatest ironists, turned on himself. Irony, like the stance of disinterestedness, is for Arnold a way of not being swallowed up by the world. He fears more than anything else the possibility that he might plunge into the "immense, moving, confused spectacle" of life, and be lost in its inauthenticity. Society is a dangerous whirlpool. "The rush and roar of practical life will always have a dizzying and attracting effect upon the most collected spectator, and tend to draw him into its vortex," and therefore man "must begin with an Idea of the world in order not to be prevailed over by the world's multitudinousness."

Arnold always keeps himself erect and aloof, like a man fording a rapid, muddy river, holding his head high and walking on tiptoe. He never has the courage to try that mode of understanding which seeks to comprehend the rationale of an alien way of life by seeing how it would feel to accept it as one's own. Arnold recognizes that this mode of understanding is an important one, and even that it is the way of knowing most proper to the poet. The poet, in order to recreate in words the spectacle of life around him, must "become what [he] sing[s]," but, whereas the Gods can with pleasure see and participate in the vast panorama of life, the poet must pay the price of great pain for his knowledge. Though the Gods cannot share human sorrows, the poet must enter fully into the sufferings as well as the joys of the heroes of his poem: "—such a price / The Gods exact for song." Being a poet seems to Arnold a matter of great suffering, the pain caused by breaking down the safe barriers of cold solitude, going outside oneself, and entering into the warmth and feeling of those who are engaged in life. Keats welcomes the chance to be "with Achilles shouting in the trenches." The more powerful the sensation the better. "Negative capability," sympathetic identification even with painful or melancholy things, is for Keats the very source of joy, of truth, and of beauty. Arnold fears such a loss of his self-possession, and goes out of himself with great reluctance. He wants to make poetry as much as possible a matter of assimilation and control rather than of diffusion and sympathy, though the process of taking the world into oneself rather than going outward into the world also seems to him a cause of suffering and effort: "For me you may often hear my sinews cracking under the effort to unite matter." Arnold fears that even this painful control over the world may be impossible. The world may slip away, rise up against the soul, and once more engulf it.

Arnold's fullest analysis of the danger of understanding through sympathy is in a famous letter to Clough. As is so often the case he projects into Clough as a *fait accompli* what he fears as a possibility for himself. Role-playing, he says, leads to a dispersal of the self, its absorption by the chaotic multiplicity of all the ways of living which society offers. "You ask me," he tells Clough, "in what I think or have thought you going wrong: in this: that you would never take your assiette as something determined final and unchangeable for you and proceed to work away on the basis of that: but were always poking and patching and cobbling at the assiette itself— could never finally, as it seemed—'resolve to be thyself'—but were looking for this and that experience, and doubting whether you ought not to adopt this or that mode of being of persons *qui ne vous valaient pas* because it might possibly be nearer the truth than your own: you had no reason for thinking it was, but it might be—and so you would try to adapt yourself to it. You have I am convinced lost infinite time in this way: it is what I call your morbid conscientiousness." Clough's conscientiousness is the tormenting awareness of the possibility that the other fellow has found the secret of inner certainty. Arnold's conscientiousness is that of the man who never takes the plunge into life because he fears all given ways of living are imposture, and will contaminate him. He is not sure that they are all false, but neither is he sure that any one of them is true, and so he loses infinite time, just as Clough, in Arnold's analysis of him, loses infinite time through being unable to take one mode of life as permanently his. No man in these damned times has a solid inner law and support for his being. In the absence of this man can neither accept society nor do without it, but must fluctuate between isolation and the halfhearted acceptance of a social role whose falseness he suspects from the start:

> Where shall [a man] fly then? back to men?—
> But they will gladly welcome him once more,
> And help him to unbend his too tense thought,
> And rid him of the presence of himself,
> And keep their friendly chatter at his ear,
> And haunt him, till the absence from himself,
> That other torment, grow unbearable;
> And he will fly to solitude again,
> And he will find its air too keen for him,
> And so change back; and many thousand times
> Be miserably bandied to and fro
> Like a sea-wave.

Arnold never really tries to reach the lost time of joy through society. The basis of his attitude toward society is an inability to believe that any social form embodies divine law, and his analysis of society, in his poetry and in his prose, is an attempt to persuade us of the truth of this presupposition. At one time society was in God's hand, but an originally good society has drifted further and further away from its holy beginning until mere empty husks are left. In terms of these husks, shells from which the spiritual vitality has departed, man in these days is forced to carry on his collective life. Social forms no longer draw strength from God, and, on the other hand, they are no longer appropriate to the life man leads. An awareness of the artificiality, the hollowness, the conventionality of present-day social forms characterizes the modern spirit: "Modern times find themselves with an immense system of institutions, established fact, accredited dogmas, customs, rules, which have come to them from times not modern. In this system their life has to be carried forward; yet they have a sense that this system is not of their own creation, that it by no means corresponds exactly with the wants of their actual life, that, for them, it is customary, not rational. The awakening of this sense is the awakening of the modern spirit."

The forms of society are laws, institutions, religion, the arts, language. Most of Arnold's prose is "criticism" in the sense that it is dedicated to showing the emptiness of one or another of these social forms. *Culture and*

Anarchy is based on the assumption that all classes of contemporary society, barbarians, philistines, and populace alike, are wrong in their claims to be divinely justified. England possesses "an aristocracy materialised and null, a middle-class purblind and hideous, a lower class crude and brutal." Rather than being "culture" in the sense of a viable human embodiment of divine truth, the three classes are, in one way or another, baseless anarchy, the anarchy, for example, of "doing as one likes," without any extrahuman justification. In the same way, at the heart of Arnold's several books on religion is the assumption that language cannot incarnate God's truth. *St. Paul and Protestantism* is an attempt to demolish the Puritan claim to speak "scientifically" about God in the language of the "covenant of redemption," "the covenant of works," "original sin," "free election," "effectual calling." The trouble with this kind of language is that it is "talking about God just as if he were a man in the next street." We can never talk about God in this way. St. Paul had the secret of righteousness and lived in harmony with God's law, but Protestantism has reduced St. Paul to empty formulas, and lives outside the divine kingdom. In the chapter in *God and the Bible* called "The God of Metaphysics" Arnold attempts to demonstrate that the central words of metaphysics, "is," "being," "essence," "existence," "substance," and so on, are derived from words for physical nature. Since they all come from terms for earthly experience, they can tell us nothing whatever about God. "*Être*," says Arnold, "really means to breathe," and to say "God is," is simply to say "God operates, . . . the Eternal which makes for righteousness has operation." Arnold assumes here that the origin of a word permanently limits its meaning. Abstract words are metaphorical extensions of concrete terms. Therefore they can never be anything but figurative. As abstractions they refer to nothing at all. All we can honestly say about God and his heaven is: "We know nothing about the matter, it is altogether beyond us."

This idea about the nature of language contains a theological implication. It assumes that God transcends our speech. He can only be defined negatively, as "not ourselves," that is, as unthinkable and therefore unspeakable. We cannot even speak of God as "He," for that is to anthropomorphize God, to think of It after the model of a "magnified and non-natural man." "It," the "not ourselves," can only be known through Its operation, as what "makes for righteousness," whatever *that* may mean. Arnold wishes to show that all our language, even the most abstract and seemingly worthy of the transcendent character of the deity, is a "throwing out" of figurative language toward something which it cannot name and has no hope of reaching. He believes in God, but he does not believe that God can be spoken about as we speak of the things of this world.

The "end and aim of all religion" is "*access to God,*—the sense of harmony with the universal order—the partaking of the divine nature," but if the language which a people speaks cannot be an embodiment of divine truth, then society itself is no mediator between man and the "universal order." Language is one of the basic matrices of society, and no society can transcend the limits of its speech.

Perhaps, Arnold sometimes feels, the divine order can be embodied in the actions of wise and just men, men who carry out God's law even though that law cannot be formulated in a code. Perhaps the course of human events is secretly ordered by a divine Providence working immanently in things. Here, as elsewhere, Arnold's ultimate experience is negative. Repeatedly in his first book of poems he returns to the theme of divine law, and each time he concludes that God's law either does not act at all in human life or acts in a way that makes God seem an unjust tyrant, placing burdens on men too heavy to bear. "Mycerinus" is based on a story in Herodotus about a wicked king who prospers while his good and law-abiding son, Mycerinus, is condemned by the inscrutable Gods to an early death. Mycerinus concludes that he was wrong to believe that "man's justice from the all-just Gods was given." The Gods, if Gods there are, are either powerless, or care nothing for man. In any case man can know nothing of the divine realm. All our talk of God's law is merely "Stringing vain words of powers we cannot see, / Blind divinations of a will supreme." So Mycerinus gives himself to revelry for the brief six years before he is fated to die. The "Fragment of an 'Antigone,' " in which Arnold wears the mask of Sophocles, picks out for imitation that part of the play which makes clearest the difficulties of obeying God's law. Both Antigone and Creon, though they act in opposite ways, think they are guided by divine law, and the result is suffering and death. Though the "order" of society is "heaven-ordain'd," that order, when it is transformed into individual experience, is so baffling that it is as if man were left on his own, "unguided," and must make "his own welfare his unswerv'd-from law." Arnold returns once again to the theme of law in "The Sick King in Bokhara." In that poem the anguish of the king who must unwillingly condemn a man to death in order to uphold the law is set against the desire of the criminal for punishment. The criminal would rather be stoned to death than remain unjustified. In these poems it is the ambiguity of divine law rather than its complete absence which is dramatized. God's command is either difficult to know, or condemns man to apparently unmerited suffering, or forces him to acts which are repugnant to his moral sense.

Later on Arnold will find it difficult to believe even in this flawed and unsatisfactory inherence of God's law in the world. *Merope,* his most elaborate attempt to achieve the "platform" of the classical, once again has at its center the theme of law. The real protagonist is Polyphontes, the usurping ruler who has seized power because he has felt himself to be the man through whom God's law can be imposed on society. Man, the most important chorus tells us, can never be sure he acts under God's direction. God's law is never unequivocally present in any society or in any man's heart, and the man who acts as if he were divinely justified takes too great a responsibility and should be condemned: "Sternly condemn the too bold man, who dares / Elect himself Heaven's destined arm."

Law, like language, religion, or established customs, is no abiding place of the divine harmony, and the man who takes the role which society offers, far from approaching his goal, merely sacrifices his life to "some unmeaning taskwork." There *is* a proper social order, but, though man would know it if he had it, he has no way to find out beforehand how to get it. It is as if man had a lock but no key, and were forced to make blindly key after key in the hope of getting the right one by accident, or, in the metaphor of "Revolutions," it is as if he had a collection of letters, given to him by God, and could make the magic word by one and only one arrangement of those letters. Man is like a magician who has forgotten the talismanic formula, and tries desperately to find it by experimentation. Though he has tried permutation after permutation of the letters, and made of each of them a culture, he knows in his heart that no one of these words has been the right one. Man's sense of the unlawfulness of all he has yet made is the cause of the decay of civilizations. Each culture, at the height of its power, is undermined by a conviction of its wrongness. Then it "droop[s], and slowly die[s]." The drive of history is a range for order, a range for order which becomes a rage for destruction when the right order is not found. Decades before Yeats or Valéry, Arnold has already their vision of history. He says his goodbye to Greece and Rome, and sees our own civilization as destined to go the way of the rest and become bits and pieces of archaeological debris.

Man as a social being is condemned to remain an outlaw, but once he could form an extrasocial relation to his fellows, the relation of love. In the epoch of harmony lovers could be transparent to one another, and see truly into one another's souls. This communion of lovers was the microcosm of the universal harmony in which it participated. Perhaps if true love could be reestablished the cosmic background of love would also be recovered. Arnold in his own life seeks this way out of the sterility and "aridity" of his existence. The record of this attempt is the Marguerite poems.

These poems are dominated by nostalgia for an epoch when each person was not yet "enisled" in the sea of life. Marguerite, on her Alpine heights, still belongs to the pastoral age, and if Arnold can love and be loved by her, he can return, through her, to the primal origin of things, for she is "a messenger from radiant climes."

The poems express Arnold's discovery that love cannot be used in this way. Only someone who already participates in the divine life of nature would be a fit mate for Marguerite. Such a man would be himself an incarnation of the universal joy:

> His eyes be like the starry lights—
> His voice like sounds of summer nights—
> In all his lovely mien let pierce
> The magic of the universe!

Unless Arnold already shares in the "magic of the universe," Marguerite will be opaque to him. Instead of permitting him access to her inner self, she will turn on him her "pure, unwavering, deep disdain," the disdain of someone who has "look'd, and smiled, and [seen him] through." Arnold is a hollow man, and because he needs from love the vitality which makes it possible to love, he is unable to love in Marguerite's way, the way of those who "bring more than they receive." Marguerite is able to love because she contains her own springs of life and joy. She rejects disdainfully the modern sort of love, in which two people, as in "Dover Beach," need one another to fill up the void in their hearts. Such modern lovers plight their troth in the face of an awareness that there is no universal Love to guarantee particular acts of love. Aloneness is now man's real condition, and love is founded on its own despair. This is a modern "existentialist" kind of love, which says: "Since there is no 'Love,' in the sense of a power transcending man, let us create love out of nothing, in spite of the insecurity and even absurdity of such love." Marguerite has no need of this kind of love, and expects the same independence from her lover. She is one of those who "ask no love, [and] plight no faith, / For they are happy as they are."

Just as Arnold must have a poet's nature first in order to write poetry, so he must participate in the universal harmony in order to create its miniature image in the intimacy of lovers, but Arnold is outside the timeless current of God's life, an island upon time's barren, stormy flow, and therefore love is impossible for him. He abandons Marguerite because he recognizes an essential lack in himself. He is "too strange, too restless, too untamed," and she is right to reject him. He is right to leave her too, for rather than being a way to his true goal, the "establishment of God's kingdom on earth," love in these bad days leads man astray and diverts him from other possible ways out of the wilderness. Love tends to present itself to Arnold under the guise of passion, as a dangerous relaxation of moral stiffness, a "hoisting up of the mainsail and letting her drive." In "A Summer Night" the alternative to giving one's life to "some unmeaning taskwork" is the mad liberty of the "freed prisoner" who sails aimlessly across the tempestuous sea of life, "With anguish'd face and flying hair / Grasping the rudder hard, / Still bent to make some port he knows not where, / Still standing for some false impossible shore." Against Clough's tendency to "welter to the parching wind," to "*fluctuate*," Arnold feels it necessary to "stiffen [himself]—and hold fast [his] rudder."

Along with this conviction that the only way to get through these bad times is aloofness and stiffness, the chin held high above the swirling waters, goes another attitude toward strong feeling. Arnold often feels guilty about his inability to abandon himself to passion: "I have had that desire of fulness without respect of the means, which may become almost maniacal: but nature had placed a bar thereto not only in the conscience (as with all men) but in a great numbness in that direction"; "I doubt whether I shall ever have heat and radiance enough to pierce the clouds that are massed round me." It may be that his "coldness" and "invincible languor of spirit" are not really good qualities at all. Though passion clouds intellectual clarity, this clarity may be the thing which is cutting him off from the divine vitality. If he could drown his lucidity in a current of powerful feeling he would find himself back in a realm where things blend in mutual interpenetration. While intellect coldly sets things against one another, and puts a void between them, feeling is a warm flow in which things lose their sharp edges, and the mind its separateness. Though speech belongs to surface life and is never authentic, the "nameless feelings that course through our breast" come from the deep buried life and share its truth. In those rare moments when the buried life is liberated and "our eyes can in another's eyes read clear" the vehicle of this possession of ourselves and of another person is not speech or intellect. It is the recovery of "a lost pulse of feeling."

Religion, in Arnold's famous definition, is "morality touched with emotion." By itself morality is not strong enough to lead man to the good. Emotion comes, though distantly and obscurely, from God, and when morality is irradiated with this gracious element of feeling it is strong enough to guide man's steps toward heaven. Creeds and dogmas are not so important as the unspeakable feeling they express, and this felling is the same whatever the creed. The fact that man is forced to use speech and concepts is merely proof of his separation from the fusing joy. In his religious books, as in his doctrine of poetry, Arnold wants to return to a time before abstract thought was necessary, a time when man lived his religion directly, in powerful feeling, without needing to think about it.

Arnold's theories of religion and love are strikingly similar, and he returns, in a religious context, to his notion that the loved one can serve as a mediator between man and God. In *St. Paul and Protestantism* he rejects the idea that Jesus is the Mediator either in the metaphysical sense of the divine Logos, or in the Old Testament sense of the Messiah. Science, he says, can neither prove nor disprove these ideas. They are something we can know nothing about. Arnold proposes as truly St. Paul's an analysis of the power of Jesus based on his own earlier theory of love between the sexes. Though there is a moral law which we should obey, by himself man is unable to know and follow this law. Jesus, alone of all men, was without sin, and He "lived to God." Ordinary men are not strong enough to reach the kingdom of God by a cold performance of duty, but if they love Jesus, then the current of emotion and sympathy binding them to Him will allow them to reach God through Jesus. Only in this sense is Jesus the Mediator: "Every one knows how being in love changes for the time a man's spiritual atmosphere, and makes animation and buoyancy where before there was flatness and dulness: . . . [Being in love] also sensibly and powerfully increases our faculties of action." When Paul loved Jesus, "appropriated" the power of Jesus, "the struggling stream of duty, which had not volume enough to bear him to his goal, was suddenly reinforced by the immense tidal wave of sympathy and emotion." What was possible for St. Paul, reaching God through his love for Jesus, is by no means necessarily possible for Arnold. Even for St. Paul this loving attachment to Jesus was faith, the "power of holding on to the unseen." For the deity is an "unseen God." In religion as in love the ideas of separation, of unavailability, are essential for Arnold. He uses here his basic metaphor of human life, the stream. Religious life, like life in general, is a moving toward a goal which transcends man, as the ocean transcends any point on the river which flows toward it.

Nevertheless, if Arnold's analyses of love and religion are correct, perhaps by abandoning himself to passion man could win at last to the promised land. In "The New Sirens" Arnold makes a sustained attempt to consider the possibility of reaching the center of reconciliation through passion. This poem, like "Parting," is oriented in terms of a vertical axis. In "Parting" Arnold rejects the downward pull of Marguerite for the sake of the "high mountain-platforms" close to the origin of things. The protagonists of "The New Sirens," on the other hand, are victims of the modern enchantresses. They have been lured away "From the watchers on the mountains, / And the bright and morning star." They have left the high morning star of intellectual truth for the opposing attraction of sexual passion. The new sirens promise to give the poet all he has sought so arduously and unsuccessfully on the mountains. Only through passion can man recover his lost proximity to God, for the heart "glean'd, when Gods were speaking, / Rarer secrets than the toiling head," and the heart is still the best avenue to divine truth: "Only, what we feel, we know."

The promise of the new sirens turns out to be false, and Arnold has already, in this early poem, rejected the strategy of reaching heaven through passion. Passion gives only a false semblance of reconciliation and unity. It is a losing of oneself which is not a finding of the new life. Even if the intoxicating sense of insight which accompanies overwhelming feeling were a true glimpse of God, it would be no more than a glimpse, for "on raptures follow calms." Passion is naturally evanescent. It cannot ever be consciously enjoyed, for to think of it destroys it. Man never realizes the benefits of passion, for he is not himself when he abandons himself to it. The life of passion, this alternation of ennui and excitement, is no way out of the sterility of these present times; "it cannot last: time will destroy it: the time will come, when the elasticity of the spirits will be worn out, and nothing left but weariness." Weariness and ennui are the fruits of strong feeling, and man finds himself, after the expense of passion, still wandering in the desert, as far as ever from the promised land. Sensual ecstasy is no substitute for the "hard and solitary" "life of the spirit." Arnold must bid his heart renounce passion forever, and return to his solitude:

> —and thou, thou lonely heart,
> Which never yet without remorse
> Even for a moment didst depart
> From thy remote and spheréd course
> To haunt the place where passions reign—
> Back to thy solitude again!

All the ways to escape from these damned times have failed. Not the exploration of time or space, not the acceptance of society, not love, not passion—no way will work, and whichever way Arnold turns he is thrown back on himself, and on his usual state of isolation and fluctuation.

Perhaps instead of struggling to get out of his situation man should accept his lot. A recurrent impulse of Arnold's spirit is the desire for calm, for immobility, for a total relaxation of effort. If all attempts to escape from his present state are hopeless, it might be possible to avoid pain by lying motionless like a stone. This would be the despairing resignation of the prisoner who, having struggled in vain against his chains, gives up trying to get free. It is this ability to accept coercion without anguish which Arnold envies in stones, trees, and stars. Nature is "mild and inscrutably calm."

Arnold also admires this ability to take what comes, not to ask anything from life, in Epictetus or Marcus Aurelius, and in such modern heroes as "Obermann." Man must, like the Stoics, "learn to wait, renounce, withdraw." How can someone who is an "aimless unallay'd Desire" achieve the calm endurance of a stone? It seems that only death will make him stonelike. Arnold does often "play dead" in his poems; he sets against a life of "turning, turning, / In mazes of heat and sound" the calm immobility of a corpse, and he longs for the corpse's peace:

> Strew on her roses, roses,
>   And never a spray of yew!
> In quiet she reposes;
>   Ah, would that I did too!

The dead, however, are out of life altogether. Arnold needs to find a way to achieve, in life, the peace of the dead. He sometimes thinks he has found a way in the notion of equilibrium, of distance, but not too great a distance, from the whirling world. If the full plunge into life puts a man at the mercy of the "mazes of heat and sound," and if a total withdrawal leads to the anguish of isolation, it might be possible to reach a point exactly in the middle, neither too close to life nor too far away from it. This strategy would be "not too near" "to men's business," but detachment would be used to comprehend that business, for through it one would "[win] room to see and hear." What would be seen would be held at arm's length, and therefore understood and controlled by the "even-balanced soul" of the spectator. This would not be as good as the true peace of a full engagement in a proper life. It would be "the second best." But the second best is better than nothing, and if the poet could find the "quiet watershed / Whence, equally, the seas of life and death are fed" it might be possible to achieve a tolerable life by remaining poised there in precarious equilibrium. Having balanced himself in this way he would have found at last, in "sad lucidity of soul," an assiette, a platform, a way to achieve fixity. From his "high station" he could "[see] life steadily, and [see] it whole."

Unfortunately, however hard he tries, Arnold cannot achieve the delicate equilibrium which has withdrawn from life to just the right distance. There is no secure platform at that spot. It is like suspending oneself in midair or balancing on a knife-edge. The pull to one side or the other is too great, and man plunges either into society or into solitude, either into life or into death. Immobility is impossible, and each man is condemned to "oscillation," to being miserably bandied to and fro like a sea-wave. The name for this perpetual wavering is "*ennui . . .* the disease of the most modern societies." Arnold draws a classic description of ennui from Lucretius: "A man rushes abroad . . . because he is sick of being at home; and suddenly comes home again because he finds himself no whit easier abroad. He posts as fast as his horses can take him to his country-seat: when he has got there he hesitates what to do; or he throws himself down moodily to sleep, and seeks forgetfulness in that; or he makes the best of his way back to town again with the same speed as he fled from it. Thus every one flies from himself."

Though Arnold tries all the ways to fly from himself, his attempts to escape lead him inevitably back to his original state of ennui. His unsuccessful flights from himself are the very causes of that state.

The failure of every effort to reach peace leads Arnold to discover the essential nature of his situation. When man dwelt in the divine kingdom he could reconcile opposites, for all qualities existed together in harmonious tension. When the world exploded into multiplicity the opposites were divided from one another. Man hungers for unity, for totality. His exploration of the world leads to the discovery that this need must be frustrated. He can have any half of each of the pairs of opposites, never both at once. Fire, ice; height, depth; isolation, society; feeling, thought; clearness, force; aridity, fluidity; too much air or too little; freedom, law; self-possession, possession of the All—man can have only one member of each of these pairs. To have one quality without its opposite is loss of selfhood, not its recovery. The antinomies can never be reconciled, and man is condemned to the either /or of the exploded world. Arnold's thought, both in its imagery and in its conceptual axes, is dominated by the theme of irreconcilable opposites, and the constant appearance of this theme is evidence of his inability to experience the world as other than broken and disintegrated. He is either too hot or too cold, either oppressed by the stuffy air of great cities or suffocating in the thin air on the mountaintop, either tormented by solitude or poisoned by the "unavoidable contact with millions of small [natures]," either alienated from himself by submission to a false law, or driven mad by an empty freedom. He hurries everywhere, like a rat in a maze, trying to find some way of life which will bring together the opposites and allow him to have the plenitude of an undivided life. Everywhere he finds one extreme or the other, never the central harmony from which all opposites flow. Arnold's search for some power or mode of existence which will mediate between himself and God has failed in every direction. It has turned out to be impossible to remain poised in a calm equilibrium. In spite of himself he falls back into one or another of the opposites and begins again the miserable process of wavering. It seems as if "only death / Can cut his oscillations short, and so / Bring him to poise. There is no other way."

One last strategy remains, self-dependence: "Resolve to be thyself; and know that he, / Who finds himself, loses his misery!" Man must cut himself off from everything outside, and seek to reach the "only true, deep-buried [self], / Being one with which we are one with the whole world." It may be that in his own vital depths man still encompasses the divine current. If he could withdraw from all superficial engagements in life he might find himself back in the streets of the celestial city. "Sink . . . in thy soul!" Arnold cries; "Rally the good in the depths of thyself!"

This movement of withdrawal means, in one direction, a total rejection of the social world as it is. Arnold hopes that this self-purification will destroy the inauthentic, and permit the authentic to be revealed. By repudiating the false selves which have engulfed him in the rush and hurry of urban life, Arnold will allow to rise up and fill his inner emptiness the deep buried self which is his real identity. At the same time this will be a possession of the "general life," the soul of the world, the All. To possess the All is at the same moment to reach God. The "spark from heaven" will fall, and man will be the source of true and fresh ideas from God, a "bringer of heavenly light." This light will illuminate human society. When man recovers his deep buried self he will himself become the mediator he has sought in vain.

The buried life is characterized by its individuality, and by the fact that to possess it coincides with possession of the totality of the world, therefore with possession of God. It is undifferentiated, like God himself, and yet it is *my* self, special to me alone. It is the self I recover when I escape from the successions of time and the divisions of space. The buried life dwells in the place where origin and ending are simultaneous. It comes from the depths of the soul in the form of floating, evanescent emotions which resist embodiment in words. It is truly a self—personal, and yet universal. To reach it would be to gain everything I lack.

In attempting to reach the buried life by cutting himself off from every contaminating influence Arnold makes his most frightening discovery, the discovery recorded in *Empedocles on Etna*. At this moment the thin strand connecting the soul to the self and the self to God's joy is being cut, and the soul is being transformed into sheer emptiness. Whether by going down toward the deep buried self and finding it "infinitely distant" in the "unlit gulph of himself," or by going up on the mountaintops toward the "unseen God," Arnold finds that by separation from everything external he gets not possession of himself, but the final loss of life and joy. Though he gets clearer and clearer, higher and higher above the turmoil of ordinary life, he does not get one inch closer to the buried self or to the divine spark. No revelation, no intuition, no presence of god is possible. What happens is a progressive evacuation of the soul, a progressive appearance of the true emptiness of consciousness. This emptiness is defined by its infinite distance from the buried self and from the divine transcendence. So Arnold writes, in "Stagirius," of the tragic situation,

> When the soul, growing clearer,
>   Sees God no nearer;
> When the soul, mounting higher,
>   To God comes no nigher.

These lines, in their very banality of rhythm and expression, are of great importance to an understanding of Arnold. No other lines express so succinctly the pathos of his spiritual experience. The prosodic slackness of the verses, and the singsong of their feminine rhymes match the terrible spiritual slackness and despondency which is their meaning. In these lines is enacted that drama of the disappearance of God which makes the nineteenth century a turning point in the spiritual history of man. When every external way back to God has failed, the soul turns within, and hopes to reach the unseen self and the unseen God through rejection, simplification, clarification, the climb to the pure heights of the soul's solitude. Surely in its most secret places the soul is still bound to God. But clarity becomes vacuity, and the soul confronts at last the horror of its own nothingness. Though Arnold should climb forever he would not move a cubit closer to God, for no progress is possible along an infinite course, and he remains, however far he goes, an empty desire.

In *Empedocles on Etna* the Greek philosopher-poet recognizes that there is still a thin strand connecting him to the universal life, a narrow channel through which he participates in the "immortal vigour" of earth, air, fire, and water. This "held-in joy" of nature shares in God's life. Empedocles possesses God through nature, but at this very moment the fragile link to God is being broken. In a final attempt to save himself from isolation while there is yet time, Empedocles plunges into the crater. He sacrifices his separate existence for the sake of a total participation in the "All," the universal life which is diffused throughout nature.

Empedocles makes the extreme choice of suicide, and saves his soul, but Arnold only imagines this possibility. His rejection of suicide and his remorse for having considered it are clear enough in his repudiation of *Empedocles on Etna* in the Preface of 1853. Arnold chooses to remain behind as a survivor into those black times which Empedocles foresees. Empedocles kills himself at the moment he is about to become "Nothing but a devouring flame of thought— / But a naked, eternally restless mind!" He knows that once a man is transformed into intelligence, he is doomed. His body will, after his death, find a home among the several elements from which it came, but mind can find no resting place in the universe. There is nothing it can blend with or find itself reflected in. The man who is all mind is condemned to wandering and solitude. He is irrevocably trapped in the prison of himself, and will remain one of "the strangers of the world."

The last consequence of man's transformation into mind is the worst of all. A man who is wholly mind is unable to die. He is doomed, as in a passage from Eastern philosophy which Arnold recorded in his notebooks, to the horror of the eternal return. His endless life will be a constant repetition of the same failure to escape from himself. He will be born again and again, and in each new reincarnation will seek frantically to be absorbed back into the general life. The elements will reject him as always, for mind is allied to none of them. He will be thrust back into life, again to seek unsuccessfully for death and its obliteration of selfhood. He will endure a perpetual transmigration, and move endlessly across the surface of existence, his "ineffable longing for the life of life / Baffled for ever." As in Kafka's terrifying story of "The Hunter Gracchus," the worst suffering is that man should seek death, and yet be unable to find it. The discovery that man may be condemned to "be astray for ever" is the climax not only of *Empedocles on Etna*, but of all Arnold's experience.

The breaking of the unity of man, nature, and God which Empedocles experienced in his time, and which Arnold experiences in ours, is not an isolated event. The moment of Empedocles' death is a true turning point or pivot of history. It is the instant when God withdraws from the world. Only at such a time does man experience himself as complete emptiness. All Arnold's frustrated attempts to escape back to the epoch when man could participate in the divine life have led him inexorably to the discovery of the truth about man's present condition: vacuity and distance are what man, in these bad times, really is. And this vacuity and distance, "the void which in our breasts we bear," can in no way be escaped.

GEOFFREY TILLOTSON

Matthew Arnold's Prose: Theory and Practice

The relation of mind and written words is a topic of long standing, and Arnold's contribution to it must serve as my excuse for making one of my own. In the process I shall draw on Arnold only here and there, reserving my fuller consideration of his theory and practice till the second half of my essay.

Our response to a piece of literature is both intellectual and aesthetic. What is intellectual in it applies itself to the content—to the matter, the way it is being thought about, the conclusions being drawn from it, the purpose it is being made to serve. If we are the best sort of reader, ready to give the author a fair hearing, the intellect starts by being passive, adjusted to watch and acquire. That state, however, cannot last long, because even the fair reader is a critic, and criticism is mental action. We become combative, for we ourselves might have written the piece—we possess a store of matter more or less similar to that being presented to us; we can think for ourselves; we have our own purposes to serve. And so we make a judgment, our judgment being the culmination of a process: as Arnold noted more than once, judgment forms insensibly as reading proceeds.

All this is in the keeping of the intellect. But already our intellectual response has extended to the aesthetic. For everything in the writer's mind exists coloured by his own individuality, the reader's experience of which colouring is an aesthetic experience. This colouring the intellect either approves or disapproves—Pater approved of the "fine atmosphere of mind" he

From *The Art of Victorian Prose*, edited by George Levine and William Madden. © 1968 by Oxford University Press.

found in Wordsworth's poetry, and George Eliot disapproved of the atmosphere she found in Pater's *Renaissance* as quite "poisonous." The intellectual and the aesthetic also act together because some part of our aesthetic response is prompted by some part of the matter that is engaging our intellect in the first place, and almost all the matter if the piece is mainly descriptive. To matter that has prompted an aesthetic response when encountered in the course of practical living we respond aesthetically all over again at the sight of the words that recall that practical experience—it seems as if we possess an outfit of shadow senses for the purpose. To take a sentence from Sir Thomas Browne as an instance—an instance brief enough to preclude any noticeable response to his strong personality: "But the iniquity of oblivion blindly scattereth her poppy, and deals with the memory of men without distinction to merit of perpetuity." Our aesthetic response to the matter of this is to a composite picture of the scattering of a liquid opiate and the generalised "idea" of a poppy. Moreover, as that same instance shows strikingly, some part of our total aesthetic response to literature is to its words as words.

When we are discussing prose apart from its content we are discussing our aesthetic response *in toto* and what prompts it. Later on I shall have something to say about our aesthetic response (joined with a response on the part of the intellect) to the colouring supplied by Arnold's personality, but neither that sort of response nor the aesthetic response to the sensuous part of the matter invites any discussion. More tricky, however, is the response we make to the words as words.

I have been using the term "literature" so far, but critics have usually restricted the operation of the aesthetic awareness of words as words to the reader of part of literature only—to literature in verse and to literature as certain sorts of prose. Coleridge so restricted it, specifying "oratory" as a sort of prose that could be ranged with literature in verse. Perhaps others besides myself look back on his remarks as on an era in our education—they illuminated what we had long been fumbling with in twilight. Here is not the place to consider them in detail. All I shall say now is that on maturer thought they throw their light on the whole of literature rather than on a part of it. For the only deep division, as I see it, falls between two sorts of reader—the "literary" readers and the rest—rather than between two sorts of writing. By "literary" readers I mean the readers for whom an author worth the name writes in the first place.

Every literary reader is aware of words on almost all occasions when words are read, and on many when words are spoken. Sometimes he is aware of them as words even when their meaning sharply affects him as a practical person. We have evidence for this in one of Wordsworth's greatest poems, his "Elegiac Verses in Memory of my Brother." In the course of the poem he recalls the arrival of the news, conveyed presumably by letter, of John's death by drowning:

> All vanished in a single word,
> A breath, a sound, and scarcely heard.
> Sea—ship—drowned—shipwreck—so it came,
> The meek, the brave, the good, was gone;
> He who had been our living John
> Was nothing but a name.

Perhaps on occasions like these we gaze at words as a temporary refuge from the things they denote, and perhaps non-literary people gaze in that way as well as literary. However that may be, literary readers make an aesthetic response to words so nearly constant that it is strange to find Coleridge mistaking a difference between degrees of obviousness for a difference of kind. He instanced the prose of Southey as prose composed of words that themselves go unnoticed: "In the very best styles, as Southey's, you read page after page, understanding the author perfectly, without once taking notice of the medium of communication." Surely a literary critic is always aware of words as words. All that varies as he turns from one piece of literature to another is the nature of the particular wording, the qualities of his own response to it, and, later on, his own powers as a worder of that response. To call on the handiest evidence: If I myself read so humble a piece of prose as one conveying instructions, I look at its wording as closely as (I hope) I look at its instructiveness. On an early page in my pocket diary I read the following: "FAINTING. If a person faints, lay him flat on the floor or on a couch. Keep the head low and apply smelling salts or sal volatile on some cotton wool under the patient's nose. Give him a glass of cold water on recovering consciousness." When I read that, I see that I should have preferred to read: "Keep his head low and apply smelling salts or sal volatile on some cotton wool to his nostrils. Give him a glass of cold water when he recovers consciousness." (I retain the order *salts . . . wool* because for practical reasons the sooner salts are mentioned the better. There are several acceptable variants of the last clause including "when he comes round.") If that instruction had been worded so as not to offend my aesthetic sense, I suspect I should have taken in its instructions more deeply (as in any event I should if I were reading it in order to deal with an actual case of fainting on the carpet before me). Even practical instructions are approached in one way by the non-literary reader, and by the literary reader in another. Certainly, I approach Southey's prose with awareness of its words as words, and so must conclude that Coleridge's account of his own experience was mistaken.

To continue these preliminary remarks, let me try to show how thought exists apart from certain aspects of the wording. The end of writing is to produce the intended effect on the mind of the reader by means of the words used. A writer capable of achieving a thought worth expression—that is, a thought of interest to a reader—has achieved a certain amount of its wording along with it. Thought either comes into being along with words—some of them, if not all—or it very soon achieves them. Some part of the final wording, however, cannot but concern the reader's aesthetic sense. For instance, if the thought is made up of a house and Jack, and their interrelation as builder and thing built, the wording could run in various ways:

> The house that Jack built
> The house which Jack built
> The house Jack built
> The house builded by Jack
> The house erected by Jack
> The house Jack erected

and so on, drawing on "domicile" and even "property," and perhaps using the verb "edify" in a rare sense, or the obsolete "edificate." We could not say that the thought had appreciably changed at any point throughout these changes of its expression. But for the purposes of aesthetic response, changes like these are important.

We can see this by examining the corrections in authors' manuscripts, or as edition follows edition. We know, for instance, that Tennyson changed the order of verb and adverb in the line

> Freedom broadens slowly down

so as to avoid the collision of sound represented by the two *s*'s. Or to take an instance from Arnold: the ending of his essay on Marcus Aurelius gave him trouble. Some of the revision represented in the printed texts—the evidence of which is set out in Professor Super's edition of the prose works—is consequent on an improved clearness of thought. The rest of it was made in the interests of expression. For instance, the text Professor Super has chosen as his copy-text is that of the 1883 edition of *Essays in Criticism*, which received Arnold's last revisions. One of its sentences reads: "And so he remains the especial friend and comforter of all clearheaded and scrupulous, yet pure-hearted and upward striving men, in those ages most especially that walk by sight, not by faith, but yet have no open vision." Both the description of the men and the ages caused Arnold trouble, but I am concerned only with the revisions in the description of the ages. In the *Victoria Magazine*, where the essay was first printed, the last phrase of that description reads: "by faith, that have no open vision." This wording was retained when the essay was included in *Essays in Criticism* (1865), but in the second edition four years later, it became: "by faith, and yet have no open vision." In the new edition of 1880 we find: "by faith, but have, nevertheless, no open vision." A change from "and" to "but" denotes a change in the thinking, but a change from "yet" to "nevertheless" denotes a change in the expression.

Because of this concern with words as words, the critic of prose wording could just as soon be a critic of the wording of poetry. The best qualification for criticising the one is a capacity to criticise the other. The things in the wording of poetry that call for criticism are more striking than those in the wording of prose—more highly coloured, more chimingly musical, more closely packed. They are also more easily recognised and familiar, for there has been much more criticism of the wording of poetry than of prose. But to be a critic of either, one must unite the humble powers that schoolchildren exercise when they triumphantly discover alliteration and the rarer powers of being aware of the whole of the aesthetic response to wording, a whole that exists almost palpably as an object. The critic has to be as much aware of his aesthetic response to wording as Arnold was of his to the shape of a Greek tragedy—in the 1853 Preface to his *Poems* he described it in terms of a group of statuary slowly approached along an avenue until the point comes when it is possessed wholly:

> The terrible old mythic story on which the drama was founded stood, before he entered the theatre, traced in its bare outlines upon the spectator's mind; it stood in his memory, as a group of statuary, faintly seen, at the end of a long and dark vista: then came the Poet, embodying outlines, developing situations, not a word wasted, not a sentiment capriciously thrown in: stroke upon stroke, the drama proceeded: the light deepened upon the group; more and more it revealed itself to the rivetted gaze of the spectator: until at last, when the final words were spoken, it stood before him in broad sunlight, a model of immortal beauty.

Readers differ in the degree to which they make and are aware of this sort of aesthetic response, but some of them make so strong a response and are so much aware of it that they may give it more attention than they are giving to what is being said. For them the wording of Southey's prose, which like

Coleridge they will place with the "very best," achieves an elegance that exists as an object before the mental eye, as the walking gait of a racehorse exists before the eyes of the body. Some readers who happen to be what are called atheists can get much pleasure out of reading Newman, even on those occasions when, to their way of thinking, he is talking nonsense. From these instances it follows that in writing of wording as a thing prompting an aesthetic response we have a firm topic.

Before looking at Arnold's practice, there are one or two further distinctions to draw. The critic of the aesthetic response to wording is not concerned with the accuracy of the words as expression. That accuracy is in the keeping of the thought. I have said that when we achieve a thought, it comes to us in some or all of the words suitable for its expression. If the thought is clear, the words will be mainly the right ones. If not, the process of improvement will usually be a process of clarifying the thought. Like many other critics, Arnold did not see this distinction. Look at his characterisation of good prose as having "regularity, uniformity, precision, balance." In that characterisation, which we shall look into more fully later on, the third term is misused. "Precision" applies to all prose as prose is wording and only to certain prose as prose is thinking. When the wording of prose is unsatisfactory, that wording still has precision. It produces a precise aesthetic impression, but a precise impression of vagueness. To exchange it for a precise impression of light, the writer would have to clear up his thought or the mental picture he is wording. Arnold's asking precision from wording is asking for what no wording can fail to provide, however difficult we should find the describing of it. What he meant to ask for was precision of thought or mental picturing.

On another occasion he fails to make a similar distinction. He is recommending an academy on the grounds that it would reduce what he called "provinciality," and is advancing the idea that "not even great powers of mind will keep [a writer's] taste and style perfectly sound and sure, if he is left too much to himself, with no 'sovereign organ of opinions,' in these matters, near him." Here "taste" is ranged alongside "style," but the instances he gives show that it is not the wording he is objecting to but the matter it is expressing, matter that exists just so because of an alleged deficiency in taste. Take his remarks on Ruskin, for instance. He begins by quoting an "exquisite" passage that shows "Mr. Ruskin exercising his genius":

> Go out, in the spring-time, among the meadows that slope from
> the shores of the Swiss lakes to the roots of their lower mountains.
> There, mingled with the taller gentians and the white narcissus,

the grass grows deep and free; and as you follow the winding mountain paths, beneath arching boughs all veiled and dim with blossom,—paths that for ever droop and rise over the green banks and mounds sweeping down in scented undulation, step to the blue water, studded here and there with new-mown heaps, filling all the air with fainter sweetness,—look up towards the higher hills, where the waves of everlasting green roll silently into their long inlets among the shadows of the pines.

"Exquisite" as the passage is, Arnold—we may note in passing—raises an objection, an objection he brings forward apologetically:

All the critic could possibly suggest, in the way of objection, would be, perhaps, that Mr. Ruskin is there trying to make prose do more than it can perfectly do; that what he is there attempting he will never, except in poetry, be able to accomplish to his own entire satisfaction: but he accomplishes so much that the critic may well hesitate to suggest even this.

Surely this is an objection raised by a theorist, one who, to use Johnson's terms, judges by "precept" rather than "perception."

In the past, it is true, the sort of matter Ruskin expressed here had usually gone into metre. Nevertheless it would not be too much to say that Ruskin had left off writing verse simply because the matter he now wished to express—matter that included his mature perception of rocks and stones and trees— could not go into metre without being falsified. Arnold should have seen that the meaning Ruskin had achieved demanded expression in prose. To demand verse of him was like asking Bach to put the matter of a recitative into an aria. Both recitative and aria are beautiful, but the one expresses matter which, being narrative, needs to be kept moving along a line, whereas the other expresses matter which, being meditative, needs to be kept circling. The beauty of the recitative is comparatively informal, and that of the aria formal.

If we look again at the passage Arnold quotes, and especially at its striking last phrase, we see pointedly that the touch of a more regular rhythm would have killed it. Arnold, as I say, must have forgotten. That he well knew about matter choosing its form is clear from his own practice. Some of his verse is formal and some comparatively informal, while some of his prose is informal and some comparatively formal. An instance of formal prose is the invocation to Oxford in the Preface to *Essays in Criticism*. According to the precept he turns on Ruskin, that invocation ought not to have been expressed in prose at all. Prose, however, was demanded by its matter,

its thought and feeling combined. Even the comparatively informal verse of
"Dover Beach" would have denied it its rightful rhythm.

It is what Arnold goes on to say, however, that contributes most to our
discussion—when he turns to a passage that he has no good word for, a
passage in which Ruskin considers the naming of some of the characters in
Shakespeare's plays:

> Of Shakespeare's names I will afterwards speak at more length;
> they are curiously— often barbarously—mixed out of various tra-
> ditions and languages. Three of the clearest in meaning have been
> already noticed. Desdemona—"δυσδαιμονία," *miserable fortune*—
> is also plain enough. Othello is, I believe, "the careful"; all the
> calamity of the tragedy arising from the single flaw and error in
> his magnificently collected strength. Ophelia, "serviceableness,"
> the true, lost wife of Hamlet, is marked as having a Greek name
> by that of her brother, Laertes; and its signification is once ex-
> quisitely alluded to in that brother's last word of her, where her
> gentle preciousness is opposed to the uselessness of the churlish
> clergy:—"A *ministering* angel shall my sister be, when thou liest
> howling." Hamlet is, I believe, connected in some way with
> "homely," the entire event of the tragedy turning on betrayal of
> home duty. Hermione (ἕρμα), "pillar-like" (ἡ εἶδος ἔχε χρυσέης
> Ἀφροδίτης); Titania (τιτήνη), "the queen;" Benedick and Bea-
> trice, "blessed and blessing;" Valentine and Proteus, "enduring
> or strong" (*valens*), and "changeful." Iago and Iachimo have evi-
> dently the same root—probably the Spanish Iago, Jacob, "the
> supplanter."

Arnold comments:

> Now, really, what a piece of extravagance all that is! I will not
> say that the meaning of Shakespeare's names (I put aside the
> question as to the correctness of Mr. Ruskin's etymologies) has
> no effect at all, may be entirely lost sight of; but to give it that
> degree of prominence is to throw the reins to one's whim, to
> forget all moderation and proportion, to lose the balance of one's
> mind altogether. It is to show in one's criticism, to the highest
> excess, the note of provinciality.

Here it is not the wording he is objecting to, but the matter, and the intellect
responsible for it. He is not speaking of prose, but of its content.

Arnold's remark about what is proper matter for prose witnesses to a limitation in his view of the function of prose. He would limit it to the expression of thinking, or, if to more than thinking, then only to the simplest narrative and description—he advised Hardy to narrate in the style Swift had used for *Gulliver's Travels,* overlooking the difference in the degree of complexity between their respective matter. Arnold thought of good prose as being one sort of prose only.

That is how Clough had thought of it in his lecture on Dryden, an excerpt of which had appeared in *Poems and Prose Remains* of 1869. Clough there had written:

> Our language before the Restoration certainly was for the most part bookish, academical, and stiff. You perceive that our writers have first learnt to compose in Latin; and you feel as if they were now doing so in English. Their composition is not an harmonious development of spoken words, but a copy of written words. We are set to study ornate and learned periods; but we are not charmed by finding our ordinary everyday speech rounded into grace and smoothed into polish, chastened to simplicity and brevity without losing its expressiveness, and raised into dignity and force without ceasing to be familiar; saying once for all what we in our rambling talk try over and over in vain to say; and saying it simply and fully, exactly and perfectly.
>
> This scholastic and constrained manner of men who had read more than they talked, and had (of necessity) read more Latin than English; of men who passed from the study to the pulpit, and from the pulpit back to the study—this elevated and elaborated diction of learned and religious men was doomed at the Restoration. Its learning was pedantry, and its elevation pretence. It was no way suited to the wants of the court, nor the wishes of the people. It was not likely that the courtiers would impede the free motions of their limbs with the folds of the cumbrous theological vesture; and the nation in general was rather weary of being preached to. The royalist party, crowding back from French banishment, brought their French tastes and distastes. James I loved Latin and even Greek, but Charles II liked French better even than English. In one of Dryden's plays is a famous scene, in which he ridicules the fashionable jargon of the day, which seems to have been a sort of slipshod English, continually helped out with the newest French phrases.
>
> Dryden then has the merit of converting this corruption and

dissolution of our old language into a new birth and renovation.
And not only must we thank him for making the best of the
inevitable circumstances and tendencies of the time, but also
praise him absolutely for definitely improving our language. It is
true that he sacrificed a great deal of the old beauty of English
writing, but that sacrifice was inevitable; he retained all that it
was practicable to save, and he added at the same time all the
new excellence of which the time was capable.

You may call it, if you please, a democratic movement in the
language. It was easier henceforth both to write and read. To
understand written English, it was not necessary first to understand Latin: and yet written English was little less instructive
than it had been, or if it was less elevating, it was on the other
hand more refining.

For the first time, you may say, people found themselves reading words easy at once and graceful; fluent, yet dignified; familiar,
yet full of meaning. To have organised the dissolving and separating elements of our tongue into a new and living instrument,
perfectly adapted to the requirements and more than meeting the
desires and aspirations of the age, this is our author's praise. But
it is not fully expressed until you add that this same instrument
was found, with no very material modification, sufficient for the
wants and purposes of the English people for more than a century.
The new diction conquered, which the old one had never done,
Scotland and Ireland, and called out American England into articulation. Hume and Robertson learnt it; Allan Ramsay and
Burns studied it; Grattan spoke it; Franklin wrote it. You will
observe that our most popular works in prose belong to it. So do
our greatest orators. A new taste and a new feeling for the classics
grew up with it. It translated, to the satisfaction of its time,
Homer and Virgil.

The style achieved by Dryden and the eighteenth-century writers generally
was the style that Arnold himself wanted to write, after adapting it, of happy
necessity, to his own genius. In his Preface to his short edition of *The Six
Chief Lives from Johnson's "Lives of the Poets"* he repeated in his own way what
Clough had said:

It seems as if a simple and natural prose were a thing which we
might expect to come easy to communities of men, and to come
early to them; but we know from experience that it is not so.

Poetry and the poetic form of expression naturally precede prose. We see this in ancient Greece. We see prose forming itself there gradually and with labour; we see it passing through more than one stage before it attains to thorough propriety and lucidity, long after forms of consummate accuracy have already been reached and used in poetry. It is a people's growth in practical life, and its native turn for developing this life and for making progress in it, which awaken the desire for a good prose,—a prose plain, direct, intelligible, serviceable. A dead language, the Latin, for a long time furnished the nations of Europe with an instrument of the kind, superior to any which they had yet discovered in their own tongue. But nations such as England and France, called to a great historic life, and with powerful interests and gifts either social or practical, were sure to feel the need of having a sound prose of their own, and to bring such a prose forth. They brought it forth in the seventeenth century; France first, afterwards England.

The Restoration marks the real moment of birth of our modern English prose. Men of lucid and direct mental habit there were, such as Chillingworth, in whom before the Restoration the desire and the commencement of a modern prose show themselves. There were men like Barrow, weighty and powerful, whose mental habit the old prose suited, who continued its forms and locutions after the Restoration. But the hour was come for the new prose, and it grew and prevailed. In Johnson's time its victory had long been assured, and the old style seemed barbarous. Johnson himself wrote a prose decidedly modern. The reproach conveyed in the phrase "Johnsonian English" must not mislead us. It is aimed at his words, not at his structure. In Johnson's prose the words are often pompous and long, but the structure is always plain and modern. The prose writers of the eighteenth century have indeed their mannerisms and phrases which are no longer ours. Johnson says of Milton's blame of the Universities for permitting young men designed for orders in the Church to act in plays: "This is sufficiently peevish in a man, who, when he mentions his exile from college, relates, with great luxuriance, the compensation which the pleasures of the theatre afford him. Plays were therefore only criminal when they were acted by academics." We should now-a-days not say *peevish* here, nor *luxuriance*, nor *academics*. Yet the style is ours by its organism, if not by its phrasing. It is by its organism,—an organism opposed to length and involvement, and enabling us to be clear, plain, and short,— that English style after the Restoration breaks with the style of the times preceding it, finds the true law of prose, and becomes modern; becomes, in spite of superficial differences, the style of our own day.

This desirable style Arnold characterises as having "regularity, uniformity, precision, balance."

I have already suggested that "precision" is a property of the thought rather than of the wording. The other three desiderata amount to no more, I think, than what was expressed by Hopkins in one word when he described his own prose (some of the best written in the nineteenth century) as "evenflowing."

II

Arnold's call for smoothness had topical point. It came more forcefully in view of Carlyle's explosiveness, and a noticeable contemporary cult of an oracular prose consisting of short sentences constructed according to the simplest of patterns. Perhaps this cult recurs periodically in the history of English prose. Thomas Reid had affected it in the mid-eighteenth century. For example: "A man of sense is a man of judgment. Good sense is good judgment. Nonsense is what is evidently contrary to good judgment. Common sense is that degree of judgment which is common to men with whom we can converse and transact business." I have shown elsewhere that a similar syntax was being favoured as the vehicle for description in verse. In prose it was also being favoured in *Ossian* for this and other purposes. More recently there had been the prose of the belletrist R. A. Willmott, who was much read, it seems, and whose *Pleasures, Objects, and Advantages, of Literature. A Discourse* appeared first in 1851 (and last in 1906). From the start he had formed his sentences, as J. A. Froude did, on the subject-verb-object pattern, but at first so disguised the pattern with additions that it was not noticeable; Froude, by those means, made a style that has been much admired. In the *Discourse*, however, Willmott pared his bi- and tri-partite sentences to the minimum. Here is a sample:

A thoughtful person is struck by the despotic teaching of the modern school. The decisions of the eighteenth century are reversed; the authority of the judges is ignored. Addison's chair is filled by Hazlitt; a German mist intercepts Hurd. Our classical writers daily recede further from the public eye. Milton is visited like a monument. The scholarly hand alone brushes the dust from Dryden. The result is unhappy. Critics and readers, by a sort of necessity, refer every production of the mind to a modern standard. The age weighs itself. One dwarf is measured by another. The fanciful lyrist looks tall, when Pindar is put out of sight.

It is plain that sentences like these, on the barest subject-verb-object pattern, do not provide a staple for extended prose, simply because of the universal law that we soon tire of the repetition of a pattern that is recognisable—the writers who used this oracular style forgot that oracles stop speaking as soon as possible. As I have said, a major writer took up the pattern but made it unrecognisable except to the analyst of wording—there is nothing jerky about Froude's style. One of the greatest, Carlyle, may be said to have made a point of cultivating jerks, but there is no monotony because he multiplied the angles from which they struck the reader.

Like most other nineteenth-century writers, Arnold was fascinated by the strange performance of Carlyle. His brilliant mimicry exists in the letters to Clough, and scraps of it persist till the end—a climax in the late essay on Gray reads as if Carlyle had worded it: "How simply said, and how truly also! Fain would a man like Gray speak out if he could, he 'likes himself better' when he speaks out; if he does not speak out, 'it is because I cannot.' "

Clearly, such prose lacked evenflowingness. The prose Arnold recommended avoided what might be called markedly varying contours, such as characterised oratorical prose. For at least two centuries now the prose written in England had been drawing away from oratory and coming nearer to conversation. In other words, the supposed distance between writer and reader was diminishing. In writing oratorical prose, the writer thinks of himself as dominating his audience from a platform. In writing conversational prose, the writer thinks of himself as on a level with it. And whereas the orator's audience is myriad, the writer of conversational prose has an audience of one. Sterne marked an important point in the history of English written prose when he noted that "Writing, when properly managed (as you may be sure I think mine is) is but a different name for conversation." That remark opens a chapter (book 2, chapter 11) of *Tristram Shandy*, and in the context "conversation" retains some of its older sense of "social intercourse"—Sterne goes on to warn the reader that he is relying on him to draw on his own experience so as to eke out what cannot be written down in all its completeness. But that the word has also much of its newer, narrower meaning is also plain—it comes in the midst of a book that is almost wholly made up of something as near as possible to the prose we talk together. The preference for written conversational prose meant first of all a looser ordering of the matter being expressed, and secondly a more intimate personal colouring, which might show itself as an addition to the matter, but which would very much affect the wording.

The approach made by written prose to conversation had been embarrassed, as Clough implied in the passage I have quoted, by the age-old habit of imitating the syntax of classical Latin. It may be that in the seventeenth century and earlier this imported syntax was as noticeable in cultivated conversation as a syntax flowing down from Anglo-Saxon. If so, manners, on which conversation depends, were soon to change. An early, and as it happened fictitious exponent of the newer style showed it at its most brilliant. The conversation of Shakespeare's most voluble personage exhibited a prose strikingly different from most of the prose being written at the time. That Hamlet was of the Court went without saying, but to the courtly he added an at least equal amount of the academical—he was also of the University. The prose he spoke and the familiar letter he wrote to Horatio (that to Ophelia belonged to a different kind) was a prose appropriate for writers who were trying to think about the new matter then coming into man's ken, and whose writings were mainly addressed to the aristocracy. We can imagine Dryden writing it, despite his remark that Shakespeare had imitated the conversation of gentlemen less well than Beaumont and Fletcher—a remark that witnesses to the rate at which manners were changing in the seventeenth century. After Dryden came Addison and Pope. Pope's conversation is represented by Spence, and his written prose by the Preface to the *Works* of 1717, of which I quote a paragraph from near the end:

> If time shall make it the former, may these Poems (as long as they last) remain as a testimony, that their Author never made his talents subservient to the mean and unworthy ends of Party or self-interest; the gratification of publick prejudices, or private passions; the flattery of the undeserving, or the insult of the unfortunate. If I have written well, let it be consider'd that 'tis what no man can do without good sense, a quality that not only renders one capable of being a good writer, but a good man. And if I have made any acquisition in the opinion of any one under the notion of the former, let it be continued to me under no other title than that of the latter.

Addison and Pope gave way to Sterne, who "managed" his conversational prose so as to make it as graceful as theirs while at the same time giving it all the informality possible. Informality, whether maximum or less, might be welcomed in a novel, but not necessarily in prose of thinking, of which there was so much in the nineteenth century. And yet after Sterne's *tour de force* even the most formal prose shed some of its pomp. In Arnold's day even Herbert Spencer yielded up all he could of his native heaviness: at the conclusion of the Preface to his epoch-making *Social Statics* (1850), he referred to certain "relaxations of style" which may "be censured, as beneath the gravity of the subject," and proceeded:

> In defence of them it may be urged, that the measured movement which custom prescribes for philosophical works, is productive of a monotony extremely repulsive to the generality of readers. That no counterbalancing advantages are obtained, the writer does not assert. But, for his own part, he has preferred to sacrifice somewhat of conventional dignity, in the hope of rendering his theme interesting to a larger number.

I might add that the conversational style had its detractors. Perhaps it was his training among the Jesuits that prompted Hopkins to relegate Newman's prose to an inferior category. In a letter to Patmore towards the close of Newman's long life, he wrote:

> Newman does not follow the common tradition— of writing. His tradition is that of cultured, the most highly educated, conversation; it is the flower of the best Oxford life. Perhaps this gives it a charm of unaffected and personal sincerity that nothing else could. Still he shirks the technic of written prose and shuns the tradition of written English. He seems to be thinking "Gibbon is the last great master of traditional English prose; he is its perfection: I do not propose to emulate him; I begin all over again from the language of conversation, of common life."
>
> You too seem to me to be saying to yourself "I am writing prose, not poetry; it is bad taste and a confusion of kinds to employ the style of poetry in prose: the style of prose is to shun the style of poetry and to express one's thoughts with point." But the style of prose is a positive thing and not the absence of verse-forms and pointedly expressed thoughts are single hits and given no continuity of style.

In making this criticism, Hopkins may have been asserting his allegiance not only to the Jesuits but to Pater, his Oxford tutor, who was deliberately writing a prose far from conversational—so far that one critic described it as prose lying in state. In a review of *Dorian Gray*, he recommended writers to write English "more as a learned language," which was to revert to the method of the Elizabethans, and in his late essay, "Style," he recommended the removal of "surplusage." That recommendation had pointed reference to a characteristic of conversational prose, which favoured the sort of expressions I shall note as frequent in Arnold's prose. Meanwhile Oscar Wilde was writing in the conversational style that is still so much with us.

Aesthetic considerations bring strange bedfellows together, and among the disciples of Sterne were Dr. Arnold and Newman. These two take us into the famous Oriel Common Room, to which, in his turn, Matthew Arnold belonged. The prose Dr. Arnold wrote, on occasions at least, is sufficiently indicated by a passage in a letter of Newman's of 1833 in which he sought an opinion about a piece of his own prose from a friend. Having applied the word "flippant" to it (in the older sense of "fluent, talkative, voluble"), he paused to gloss it with "by which I mean what Keble blames in [Dr.] Arnold's writings, conversational." If Newman was uncertain whether or not he had gone too far, it was down a favourite path—he would any day have preferred the flippant to the pompous: there was nothing in him of "stained-glass attitudes," to use Gilbert's brilliant phrase. Froude has left us a picture of Newman's bearing in conversation.

> He, when we met him, spoke to us about subjects of the day, of literature, of public persons and incidents, of everything which was generally interesting. He seemed always to be better informed on common topics of conversation than any one else who was present. He was never condescending with us, never didactic or authoritative; but what he said carried conviction along with it. When we were wrong he knew why we were wrong, and excused our mistakes to ourselves while he set us right. Perhaps his supreme merit as a talker was that he never tried to be witty or to say striking things. Ironical he could be, but not ill-natured. Not a malicious anecdote was ever heard from him. Prosy he could not be. He was lightness itself—the lightness of elastic strength—and he was interesting because he never talked for talking's sake, but because he had something real to say.

Newman's manners are the key to his prose, and to that of Matthew Arnold also. For this purpose we need go no further, in amplification of Froude, than to Clough's oblique description of them in a description of Emerson, who was then on a visit to Oxford:

> Everybody liked him. . . . He is the quietest, plainest, unobtru-
> sivest man possible—will talk but will rarely *discourse* to more
> than a single person—and wholly declines "roaring." . . . Some
> people thought him very like Newman. But his manner is much
> simpler.

Newman managed his elaborate simplicity with deftness. His grace was
crisp. But his horror of being "abrupt" was as strong as his horror of being
pompous. His walk was as near to a swift gliding as feet and cassock could
make it. We know that he never raised his voice, relying on his audience's
intent wish to catch what he was saying for his power of reaching them.
Over the course of his long life he said much about writing, and all of it
penetrates deep. I need quote only two of his remarks.

When J. B. Mozley was embarking on his first article for the *British
Critic*, Newman, his former tutor and editor of the magazine, advised him
about the sort of prose he ought to write: "In what you write do not be too
essayish: i.e., do not begin, 'Of all the virtues which adorn the human
breast!'—be somewhat conversational, and take a jump into your subject.
But on the other hand avoid abruptness, or pertness. Be *easy* and take the
mean—and now you have full directions how to write. (The last remark is
jocular—Newman never liked assuming authority, even when he possessed
it *ex officio* or by virtue of his genius.) Then there is his description of the
notes to his translation of Athanasius: "They are written *pro re natâ*, capri-
ciously, or at least arbitrarily, with matter that the writer happens to have
at hand, or knows where to find, and are composed in what may be called
an undress, conversational style." The metaphor was academic— on ordinary
occasions a Doctor of Theology wore an M.A. gown of black instead of his
formal scarlet. Newman's style was often in "undress," if we recall how neat
and commodious an M.A. gown is. He reserved a more formal style for
such occasions as forbade the informal—as when he composed his towering
"character" of God. Those occasions were few and far between, but only
because he chose to make them so. Most of his writing was *"pro re natâ"*
because he could rely on the quality of his thinking whenever pen was set
to paper. His thinking was a flowing spring which, in view of its source,
justified itself in being just that, not needing to organise and formalise itself
into "ornamental waters." Froude tells us how well Newman could think in
conversation, but he preferred thinking, pen to paper: "I think best when I
write. I cannot in the same way think when I speak. Some men are brilliant
in conversation, others in public speaking, others find their minds act best

when they have a pen in their hands." When he wrote, however, he wrote as he would have spoken in conversation if he had come up to his own high standards for such speech. And if what he first wrote needed much correction—as it always did and which it always got—the changes were as much for the sake of grace of wording as of the revision of the thought.

We can see the appropriateness of a conversational prose for the nineteenth century. That age looked to its writers for help in understanding the universe as it was then being found to be, and for encouragement to do the good deeds that were urgently required if bloody revolution were to be averted by the narrowing of the gap between the Two Nations. In that age of crisis those many who were puzzled and troubled looked to writers for help. They earnestly wanted to hear the opinions of men they honoured, men of genius, "heroes," and to have received them in prose of a formal style would have been chilling if not insulting. They wanted advice by word of mouth. Literature was constantly spoken of at this time as a voice. At the best it was an actual voice, for many of the great writers performed on platforms as lecturers. Even as lecturers they spoke conversational prose, and when their words were available only in printed pamphlet or book, conversational prose was even more welcome. Conversational prose was the nearest thing to the heard human voice.

III

Newman's sister Harriett noted that those who admired him came to write like him. That was Arnold's double fate—we have recently had a thorough examination of the long master-pupil relationship from Professor DeLaura, on the score both of manner and matter (Professor DeLaura goes into the inspiration Arnold found in Newman's ideas not only on culture but, more strangely, on religion). Arnold himself was proud to acknowledge the twofold debt, which, he confessed, people had noticed. What mainly concerns us here is his debt for authorial personality since this had its effect on the wording as well as the matter of Arnold's prose.

Arnold tried to be as like Newman as possible without ceasing to be himself. He came to think that he was more like him than Newman could allow. That he could think so showed how little he understood Newman, who was a churchman first and last and wholly, and who had even doubted if Arnold's father was a Christian. Arnold was spared a sharp reply such as Newman made on occasion, when his urbanity was simply so much polish on the blade. Arnold liked wielding the rapier more than Newman did.

There was relish to his reference to "the controversial life we all lead," whereas Newman lamented that the age afforded no time for "*quiet* thought."

And yet Arnold found in Newman's occasional sharpness the inch he extended into an ell. The manner of writing sharply he learned mainly from certain small things of Newman, the chief of which was the series of seven letters printed anonymously in *The Times* during February 1841, and soon collected in pamphlet form as *The Tamworth Reading Room.* They show Newman at the peak of his brilliance—when he found occasion to quote from them in the *Essay in Aid of a Grammar of Assent* thirty years later, he ascribed to them "a freshness and force which I cannot now command." Arnold knew these letters well, as we learn from the quotations from them entered into his notebooks. In them Newman came near to cutting a dash—anonymously, except for those who knew his authorship. Here is the opening of the sixth Letter to serve as a sample of the conversational writing that attracted Arnold: "People say to me, that it is but a dream to suppose that Christianity should regain the organic power in human society which once it possessed. I cannot help that; I never said it could." And which Arnold adopted. This comes towards the close of "The Function of Criticism at the Present Time":

> But stop, some one will say; all this talk is of no practical use to us whatever; this criticism of yours is not what we have in our minds when we speak of criticism; when we speak of critics and criticism, we mean critics and criticism of the current English literature of the day; when you offer to tell criticism its function, it is to this criticism that we expect you to address yourself. I am sorry for it, for I am afraid I must disappoint these expectations.

And so on. The likeness to conversational speech is shown in little by Arnold's preference, which he shared with Newman, for beginning his paragraphs—let alone his sentences—with abrupt monosyllables. In this same essay five begin with "But," three with the conjunctive "For," and one each with "Nay," "Or," "Still," and "Again." In the Academies essay two paragraphs begin with the exclamation "Well," one being a "Well, then," and the other "Well, but." And in the passage about Ruskin I quoted earlier, Arnold's comment, it will be recalled, began with "Now, really."

Arnold designed his authorial personality to be striking, and his prose to match—a thoughtful critic must have pleased him by describing his style in 1883 as "perhaps, more striking than that of almost any other writer at the present time." In his first prose piece Arnold was striking partly by being superior. He aired his intellectual superiority in such runs of wording as these: "What is *not* interesting, is . . . ," and " 'The poet', it is said, and by an apparently intelligent critic . . ." (in reprinting, Arnold dropped the insulting "apparently"), which is followed by "Now this view I believe to be completely false" (where the "Now" is an aggravation); a little later comes "And why is this? Simply because . . . ," and "No assuredly, it is not, it never can be so"; and again: "A host of voices will indignantly rejoin . . ."; and still again: "For we must never forget . . ." (he uses "we" but the guiltily forgetful reader knows at whom the finger is pointing). These things are more wholly wording than matter—they exhibit the manner of the egoist living in an age of controversy. That manner exists also in the many conversational intensives that Pater would have reckoned "surplusage"—"very," "signal," "very signal," "quite," "really," "profoundly." Along with these intensives go the vivid slang words, chief among which was "adequate," a term he had learned at Oxford. Near to slang are other informalities Newman had given him the taste for—homely expressions like "got talked of " and homely imagery, such as (to draw on "The Literary Influence of Academies"): "that was a dream which will not bear being pulled about too roughly," and "We like to be suffered to lie comfortably in the old straw of our habits, especially of our intellectual habits." I may also note that, like Newman, Arnold prefers that when he strikes out an important phrase it shall be quiet rather than brilliant, as Carlyle's and Ruskin's mainly were— quiet phrases like "the dialogue of the mind with itself " (from the 1853 Preface) and "doing as one likes" (a chapter heading from *Culture and Anarchy*).

Slang, homely and quiet phrases, and homely imagery combine two qualities that Arnold liked to combine—the unassuming and the striking. He liked to blend two opposed aesthetic constituents, which can be variously described. His sentences are both suave and obstructed, smooth and attitudinising, flowing and striking, urbane and barbarous. They have as much of each kind as can coexist in a state of blendedness. They move easily, but among carefully placed obstacles. Newman described the gentleman as one who "never inflicts pain," and who "carefully avoids whatever may cause a jar or a jolt." Arnold's prose has it both ways by alternating long stretches of the gentleman with a flash here and there of the *enfant terrible*. He gives jars and jolts but so deliberately that we accept them as forming part of an individual version of the gentlemanly. To read him is to watch a performance of one who comes near to inflicting pain either without actually doing so, or with ointment so smartly applied that the sting melts away. Later on I shall qualify this description a little, but it is true in the main. The reader is confident that the writer knows where he is going, whatever bundles of sub-clauses, elaborate adverbs and detachable phrases are thrust into his open arms as he moves ahead. It may have been partly this spikiness of Arnold's that led R. H. Hutton to characterise his prose as "crystal," that of Newman's being "liquid."

Take as a handy instance of all this that note Arnold appended to the first paragraph of "The Function of Criticism at the Present Time" when it was collected in his *Essays in Criticism:*

> I cannot help thinking that a practice, common in England during the last century, and still followed in France, of printing a notice of this kind,—a notice by a competent critic,—to serve as an introduction to an eminent author's works, might be revived among us with advantage. To introduce all succeeding editions of Wordsworth, Mr. Shairp's notice might, it seems to me, excellently serve; it is written from the point of view of an admirer, nay, of a disciple, and that is right; but then the disciple must be also, as in this case he is, a critic, a man of letters, not, as too often happens, some relation or friend with no qualification for his task except affection for his author.

Here there are two sentences with eleven interpolations of one sort and another.

That note also serves to illustrate another characteristic of Arnold's wording. Its flowingness is often secured by the use of the lubricating devices I have already mentioned—"I cannot help thinking," "it is permitted that," and the rest. Spikiness exists in the run of the words in "might, it seems to me, excellently serve," where we not only have the severing of auxiliary from verb but the wide severing across a clause and an adverb —an adverb that is itself spiky because of its smart latinity and ticking polysyllables. In the second paragraph of the same essay we get: "should, for greater good of society, voluntarily doom."

The main means of Arnold's strikingness is this sort of unusual word-order. In the first paragraph of the essay I am drawing my instance from we have the striking word-order of "for now many years," but the expected word-order is often rearranged if not to that degree of strikingness:

> Many objections have been made to a proposition which, in some remarks of mine on translating Homer, I ventured to put forth; a proposition about criticism, and its importance at the present day. I said: "Of the literature of France and Germany, as of the intellect of Europe in general, the main effort, for now many

years, has been a critical effort; the endeavour, in all branches of knowledge, theology, philosophy, history, art, science, to see the object as in itself it really is." I added, that owing to the operation in English literature of certain causes, "almost the last thing for which one would come to English literature is just that very thing which now Europe most desires,—criticism;" and that the power and value of English literature was thereby impaired.

Sometimes his inversions become ludicrous—sometimes he does *not* avoid paining us! I have noted elsewhere that

> his article "The Bishop and the Philosopher" has one paragraph beginning "The little-instructed Spinoza's work could not unsettle . . ." and another beginning "Unction Spinoza's work has not. . . ." If he had been more conversant with Dickens's novels he might have been warned by Mrs. Micawber's example: " 'We came,' repeated Mrs. Micawber, 'and saw the Medway. My opinion of the coal trade on that river, is, that it may require talent, but that it certainly requires capital. Talent, Mr. Micawber has; capital, Mr. Micawber has not.' "

And Arnold can pain us by making a sentence carry too many weights—as in this from one of his ecclesiastical essays:

> But as it is the truth of its Scriptural Protestantism which in Puritanism's eyes especially proves the truth of its Scriptural church-order which has this Protestantism, and the falsehood of the Anglican church-order which has much less of it, to abate the confidence of the Puritans in their Scriptural Protestantism is the first step towards their union, so much to be desired, with the national Church.

A small instance of his deliberate clumsiness comes at the opening of this same essay: "I daresay this is so; only, remembering Spinoza's maxim that the two great banes of humanity are self-conceit and the laziness coming from self-conceit, I think. . . ." Surely it would have been better to write "coming from it" or "that comes of it," better because we stress the ending of a phrase and so here stress the unimportant word, the repeated "self-conceit." Arnold did not make enough use of our pronouns.

This clumsy but deliberate repetition introduces the most notorious item in Arnold's method of wording—his liking for repeating a word or phrase over and over again. For instance, having designed "regularity, uniformity, precision, balance" as a description of the prose achieved by the eighteenth century, he repeats it six times in the course of one (long) paragraph. Such repetition of invented terms is part of his method, but ill-advisedly so. He goes to ungentlemanly lengths in repeating them—his insistence has something of the *entêté* about it. This was a mistake Newman would not have made. Very occasionally Newman did repeat a word mercilessly, as for instance here:

> Again, as to the Ministerial Succession being a form, and adherence to it a form, it can only be called a form because we do not see its effects; did anything *visible* attend it, we should no longer call it a form. Did a miracle always follow a baptism or a return into the Church, who would any longer call it a form? that is, we call it a form, only so long as we refuse to walk by *faith*, which dispenses with things visible. Faith sees things not to be forms, if commanded, which seem like forms; it realizes consequences. Men ignorant in the sciences would predict no result from chemical and the like experiments; they would count them a form and a pretence. What is prayer but a form? that is, who (to speak generally) sees any thing come of it? But we believe it, and so are blessed. In what sense is adherence to the Church a form in which prayer is not also? The benefit of the one is not seen, nor of the other; the one will not profit the ungodly and careless, nor will the other; the one is commanded in Scripture, so is the other. Therefore, to say that Church-union is a form, is no disparagement of it; forms are the very food of faith.

It is one thing, however, to repeat a monosyllable, and another to repeat a mouthful. Arnold's repeated things are often whole phrases. It may be that his habit was partly encouraged by his love for Homer. He knew the old epics more closely than any other text, except the Bible—in his lectures on translating them he mentions that for two years they were never out of his hands. Homer sometimes repeats a word of great length, and it happens that a note in Pope's translation provides a comment on Arnold's practice. Pope's seventh note on *Iliad* 19 reads:

> VERSE 197 [of his translation]. The *stern* Aeacides *replies*.] The *Greek* Verse is
>
> Τὸν δ' ἀπαμειξόμενος πζοσέφη πόδας ὠκὺς 'Αχιλλεύς.
>
> Which is repeated very frequently throughout the Iliad. It is a very just Remark of a *French* Critick, that what makes it so much

taken notice of, is the rumbling Sound and Length of the Word ἀπαμειξόμενος: [*replies*]: This is so true, that if in a Poem or Romance of the same Length as the Iliad, we should repeat *The Hero answer'd*, full as often, we should never be sensible of that Repetition. And if we are not shock'd at the like Frequency of those Expressions in the Æneid, *sic ore refert, talia voce refert, talia dicta dabat, vix ea fatus erat*, &c. it is only because the Sound of the *Latin* Words does not fill the Ear like that of the Greek ἀπαμειξόμενος.

Pope then proceeds to discuss the modern preference for avoiding the repetition of words, especially of polysyllabic words, and decides that "Either of these Practices is good, but the Excess of either vicious." In Arnold the repetitions are therefore vicious.

There is no offence, however, in what is as common in Arnold as his repeated phrases—his use of long words derived from Greek or Latin, and which if they are repeated, are not noticed as being so. They combine with the other spikinesses to enliven the general flowingness. To draw on a few pages at the beginning of the same essay on Academies we get "prominently," "pre-eminence," "nascent," "instrument," which are sprinkled here and there among the shorter Saxon words that carry the main burden of the thinking. Once Arnold ended an essay with one of these consciously favoured words. In the course of this same essay on Academies he invented a new sense for the epithet "retarding," the sense of slackening the pace of *intellectual* advance, and so can rely on the last word of his essay to come as a climax:

> He will do well constantly to try himself in respect of these, steadily to widen his culture, severely to check in himself the provincial spirit; and he will do this the better the more he keeps in mind that all mere glorification by ourselves of ourselves or our literature, in the strain of what, at the beginning of these remarks, I quoted from Lord Macaulay, is both vulgar, and, besides being vulgar, retarding.

What was desiderated for the conversational style may be described as "lightness." It may come as a surprise to some that the word "light" was one of those greatly favoured in the mid-nineteenth century. Froude, we recall, called Newman "lightness itself," and Arnold begins one of his greatest poems with

> Light flows our war of mocking words.

When his *Essays* came out he hoped that Frederick Locker-Lampson would think its Preface "done with that *light hand* we have both of us such an affection for." They were trying to make the English language more like music composed for that still fairly new instrument, the piano. Gide was to describe French prose as like a piano without pedals. We know how much Arnold admired French prose, but there is something about the English language that prevents its sounding like the amputated instrument of Gide's comparison. Newman and Arnold wanted their prose to be like a piano *with* a sustaining pedal, playing music—shall we say as like the favourite parts of Schubert's as possible, light, airy, flowing, wiry, pale-coloured, preferring to tinkle rather than to pound.

I have said that we make an aesthetic response to the personality shown in writing and that we judge it by the exercise of the intellect. Our aesthetic response to Arnold's authorial personality is one of pleasure tempered by intellectual doubt as to whether or not its pleasantness for the twentieth century was pleasantness for the nineteenth. For some nineteenth-century readers it was decidedly that—Arnold had his numerous admirers. Those admirers, however, were already, we guess, in possession of the sweetness and light he was recommending. To the "elphantine main body" of the bourgeoisie that Arnold was out to transform, he cannot have meant very much. He sometimes used the term that Hazlitt had introduced into the critical vocabulary—"tact." But how little of it he himself exercised! *Culture and Anarchy* was met with critics who saw its author as a mere aesthete looking rather out of place in the daily throng of English business: Henry Sidgwick, for instance, ridiculed him as a person "shuddering aloof from the rank exhalations of vulgar enthusiasm, and holding up the pouncet-box of culture betwixt the wind and his nobility." They might have stomached his urbanity if it had been like that of Newman—an, as it were, unconscious urbanity. They could not take the urbanity of one who postured. It seems that he made a big strategical mistake. The writer who had most effect on English culture was William Morris. For him urbanity was fluff and nonsense—unlike Arnold, he was once mistaken for a sea-captain. But if Arnold was bent on being urbane, he ought to have kept his urbanity more like Newman's, which always seemed to exist by right of second nature.

G. WILSON KNIGHT

"The Scholar-Gipsy"

Much of the poetry which we think we know best stands in need, today, of reinterpretation. By taking a wider view than has been customary, we can often expose a new vein of meaning in a well-known work which has hitherto eluded observation. Especially must we be prepared to follow Sherlock Holmes's advice by giving particular attention to any elements which appear to be intrusions, or irrelevancies, since these can often point us to a final understanding.

So advised, we may find ourselves drawn to ask whether the long simile with which Matthew Arnold ends "The Scholar-Gipsy" is organic, or merely an over-elaborated device to give us a smooth conclusion. The extended description of the Oxus at the end of *Sohrab and Rustum* carries overtones as a symbolism of life, from youthful impetuosity to complexity and tragedy, and so out to the sea of death, which are relevant to the preceding narrative. Can we say the same of the conclusion to "The Scholar-Gipsy?"

The simile of the Tyrian trader has been prepared for by an earlier, shorter, simile of the same kind. Arnold's Scholar, we may remember, is contrasted with the thought and society of the nineteenth century, which he is urged to avoid:

> Still fly, plunge deeper in the bowering wood!
> Averse, as Dido did with gesture stern
> From her false friend's approach in Hades turn,
> Wave us away, and keep thy solitude.
>
> (l.207)

From *Neglected Powers: Essays on Nineteenth and Twentieth Century Literature.* © 1971 by G. Wilson Knight. Barnes & Noble Books, 1971.

Dido, Queen of Carthage, a colony of Tyre, is a figure of feminine appeal and oriental glamour who failed to distract Aeneas from fulfilling his destiny as the founder, through Rome, of western efficiency and organization. She, like the Scholar, is a wraithly personality, and, like him, has slight respect for the values to which Aeneas, and his descendants in Arnold's day, were dedicated. This simile touches the ascendancy of Rome; and our main, concluding, simile, pushing back yet farther into the origins of our western tradition, the ascendancy of Greece. Both involve Tyre, and both are used with exact reference to the Scholar.

Here are our two final stanzas, with certain important words italicized:

> Then fly our greetings, fly our speech and smiles!
> —As some *grave* Tyrian trader, from the sea,
>   Descried at sunrise an emerging prow
> Lifting the cool-hair'd creepers *stealthily*,
>   The fringes of a southward-facing brow
>   Among the Aegean isles:
> And saw the *merry* Grecian coaster come,
>   Freighted with amber grapes, and Chian wine,
>   Green bursting figs, and tunnies steep'd in brine;
> And knew *the intruders on his ancient home*,
>
> The young *light-hearted* Masters of the waves;
>   And snatch'd his rudder, and shook out more sail,
>   And day and night held on *indignantly*
> O'er the blue Midland waters with the gale,
>   Betwixt the Syrtes and soft Sicily,
>   To where the Atlantic raves
> Outside the Western Straits, and unbent sails
>   There, where down cloudy cliffs, through sheets of foam,
>   *Shy* traffickers, the dark Iberians come;
> And on the beach undid *his corded bales*.
>
>   (l.231)

On these stanzas there is much to say.

In driving the Tyrian traders before them the Greeks established their mastery of the Mediterranean: it was the first step in a story whose sequels were the defence of Greece against the Persians, culminating in Salamis; the conquests of Alexander; and the unsuccessful challenge of Carthage, originally a Tyrian colony, against Rome. It was, therefore, the first step in establishing the western, or European, tradition, as we know it.

But there are other, more ancient, traditions, and these the Tyrians represent. The words "grave," "intruders on his ancient home," and "indig-nantly" suggest a spiritual authority recalling Shakespeare's "We do it wrong, being so majestical . . ." (*Hamlet*, 1.1.143). In contrast, the Greek moves "stealthily"; he is tricky. He is also, in this period, at the birth of our European story, called "merry" (l.237), "young" and "light-hearted" (l.241); that is, carefree, with suggestions of youthful bravery and, perhaps, irresponsibility.

As the Tyrian flies the Greek, so the Scholar is told to fly the society of nineteenth-century Europe existing within the tradition inaugurated by Greece and Rome. As he fled to the Gipsies, so the Tyrian flies to the Iberians. They are called "shy" (l.249), a word elsewhere associated with the Scholar (ll.70, 79). The undoing of the "corded bales" makes a firm conclusion, leaving us with a fine sense of secret goods, well protected, weighty, and of value. You see the dark-eyed traffickers eagerly awaiting the disclosure.

Either this is all an irrelevant decoration or we must suppose that the poem which it is there to elucidate possesses a corresponding weight and depth. But in *The Common Pursuit* F. R. Leavis argues that "The Scholar-Gipsy," though a "charming" poem, throughout pretends to be very much more than it is; that the Scholar's "one aim, one business, one desire" (l.152) is insufficiently defined; and that the poem has little to offer regarding the serious engagements of our existence. On the premises of contemporary criticism, that may be a natural conclusion. Nevertheless, those of us who are moved by Arnold's poem will not readily subscribe to it; and if we return to the text with the concluding simile in mind, we should be able to dem-onstrate its inadequacy.

We must accordingly search within the main body of the poem for qualities roughly corresponding to the oriental powers symbolized by the Tyrian trader. The Scholar is a young man of originality and brilliance (l.34), who, in a mood of dissatisfaction with the prospects offered him, leaves Oxford in comparative immaturity to join the Gipsies. His state is one of youth, "fresh, undiverted to the world without" (l.162). Official studies he has repudiated, and gone off "roaming the countryside, a truant boy" (l.198). He lives with something more than the immortality of a literary creation, "living as thou liv'st on Glanvil's page" (l.159), enjoying an "im-mortal lot" and "exempt from age" (ll.157–58) precisely because he has left the world with "powers" (l.161) untainted. We may call him the "eternal undergraduate."

He moves ghostlike about the Oxford countryside. He has "dark vague eyes and soft abstracted air" (l.99), and is called "pensive," "in a pensive dream" (ll.54, 77). He is elusive, averse from social contact, preferring "shy retreats" and "shy fields" (ll.70, 79), "retired ground" (l.71) and "solitude" (l.210). But there is nothing weak about him: he is "rapt" (l.119), that is dedicated, almost as in a trance, to an expectance defined as the "spark from Heaven" (l.120), for which he is always waiting. Nor is his life easy. While his former companions live *below* in warmth, at least part of what Dr. Leavis calls his "eternal week-end" is an arduous enough existence, a spiritual battling, on the snow-driven hills:

> And once, in winter, on the causeway chill
>> Where home through flooded fields foot-travellers go,
>>> Have I not pass'd thee on the wooden bridge
>> Wrapt in thy cloak and battling with the snow,
>>> Thy face towards Hinksey and its wintry ridge?
>>>> And thou hast climb'd the hill
>> And gain'd the white brow of the Cumner range,
>>> Turn'd once to watch, while thick the snowflakes fall,
>>> The line of festal light in Christ-Church hall—
>> Then sought thy straw in some sequester'd grange.
>
> (l.121)

Sometimes we need to read poetry with what might be called a "stage" eye; to produce it, as it were, for our own advantage; to allow it all the visual spatial significance that it can carry, and to read that significance in depth. If we accord this stanza such a reading, we shall begin to understand that the Scholar is more than a renegade from the established tradition. He is that certainly; but he is also a sentinel on the heights, an outpost of learning; more, we may even begin to see him as the presiding genius, the over-watching and guardian spirit, of Oxford, of the university.

It is right that such a guardian deity should be, not a don, but one of "glad perennial youth" (l.229); one who is eternally immature. The don has knowledge; he is a pillar of the established tradition; he probably holds academic honours. It is possible to have, and be, all this, and lack wisdom; more, it is extremely hard to have all this, and preserve wisdom; for you cannot buy wisdom with less than wonder. But in the undergraduate you have, or should have, the essence of true learning; the opening of the mind, the wonder, the intuition of fields unexplored. That is why the presiding deity of a great university may be felt as the eternal undergraduate.

But what of the Gipsies? Gipsies are supposed to possess occult abilities. The word "gipsy" derives from "Egyptian"; gipsies are, in fact, of Hindu origin; and on both counts they may be associated with the mysterious arts and wisdom of the East. In "The Scholar-Gipsy" we are told that they have "arts" of a strange sort able to rule "the workings of men's brains"; and the Scholar means, when he has mastered the secret of this magic, to offer it to mankind, presumably in terms that our western culture would understand (ll.44–50). The secret of these "strange arts" (l.135) is clearly supposed to be a great good: the Scholar expects to play the part of a benefactor.

What, more exactly, is intended? We may relate the conception to that of Wordsworth's *Recluse* fragment (printed in the preface to *The Excursion*), with its emphasis on "the mind of Man" as the "haunt" and "main region" of his "song." "Mind" and "thought" are important and power-bearing concepts in both Byron (e.g., the "eternal spirit of the chainless mind" in the Sonnet on Chillon) and Shelley. They must be regarded less as registering faculties than as active powers. As Hamlet tells us, "There is nothing either good or bad but thinking makes it so"; and in Shelley's *Prometheus Unbound* man's liberated state is one where evil and suffering, though still present, are mysteriously changed, like wild beasts tamed, so that "none knew how gentle they could be" (4.4.404–5). Certainly the liberation of dormant faculties able to modify or control our mental experience might go far to solve the human enigma.

Such possibilities have, throughout the ages, been the concern of the esoteric schools originating from the East, though certain famous Europeans, such as Swedenborg, Goethe, Blake, Rudolf Steiner, Gurdjieff, and today John Cowper Powys, have enjoyed direct experience of them. Traces of such a wisdom may be discovered, on the level of symbolism, within a great deal of our western poetry. The wisdom in question is, however, less easily mastered than the traditional learning of the West, since it aspires to be an active, and directly affective, power, and its exercise may involve arduous training and discipline. Or again, it may appear to function at choice moments without these, as though by the grace of God; and that is why the Scholar says that "it needs heaven-sent moments for this skill" (l.50).

The Scholar who is to personify the striving for such a wisdom is presented as one of "glad perennial youth" (l.229); and much of what he symbolizes is probably best understood by us in youth, before the "clouds of glory" have dissolved, before education has fitted on us its straitjacket, and conditioned us for all those "exacting" demands which Dr. Leavis complains that our Scholar, as indeed he does, repudiates. Among those likely to see the Scholar there is accordingly a high proportion of youthful persons. He gives flowers, but without speaking, to the maidens who have been engaging in May dances (ll.81–90); and we have elsewhere "boys" (l.64) and "children" (l.105). He is also seen by such simple people as shepherds (l.57), the "smock-frock'd boors" (l.59), and the "housewife" of a "lone homestead" (l.101), and by the blackbird (l.116). He may be glimpsed, too, by others enjoying active contact with nature, such as the "riders blithe" (l.72) and the bathers (l.95). On the most important occasion of all, it is the poet himself who sees him battling with the snow, and looking down on the Oxford lights (ll.121–29).

To men he remains elusive: his whole being is set on the "spark" (ll.120, 171, 188). The word "spark" is interesting. It and "brains" (l.46) are our only two *verbal* keys to the central mystery.

"Spark" is a word of some authority. Byron was fond of it. *The Curse of Minerva* (l.165) contains a caustic comment on a man "without one spark of intellectual fire"; in *Manfred*, the "mind," "spirit," or "Promethean spark" in man can challenge the elements (1.1.154); in *Don Juan* the "mind" is "a fiery particle" (11.60); and revolutionary ardour is a "spark" (*Journal*, January 9, 1821). Related examples are given in my *Lord Byron: Christian Virtues* and in *Byron and Shakespeare*. In Byron the word is a nucleus for a cluster of valuable associations which can be regarded as summed up in Browning's "finish'd and finite clods, untroubled by a spark," in "Rabbi Ben Ezra." The word has esoteric authority as the divine spark in man, the Sanskrit *atman*. It is a faculty, or power, lodged within and awaiting development, to be fanned into a blaze of total illumination. Arnold's use of "fall" in "waiting for the spark from Heaven to fall" (l.120) may, I think, be criticized: he appears to have forced together conceptions deriving respectively from the *atman* and Christian orthodoxy. The Scholar is surely waiting for the spark to be awakened rather than to fall. But we must not call the word "spark" itself a vague or ill-defined image, since it has an honourable pedigree. It is just because it has precise traditional connotations that we are aware of a discrepancy in "fall." There may even be a point in the discrepancy, since it serves as a symptom, or symbol, of the poem's total meaning, which strives, as its title "The Scholar-Gipsy" as good as tells us, towards a fusion of two traditions, western and eastern.

The main emphasis is on this very striving. Both the Scholar himself and the culture with which the poet contrasts him are shown as awaiting the revelation. But there is a distinction. He is contrasted with those

> Whose insight never has borne fruit in deeds,
> Whose vague resolves never have been fulfill'd.
>
> (l.174)

This stanza suggests throughout a state of not-being, false starts, and continual disappointment, in a retrogressive and retrospective existence without purpose, recalling Macbeth's "all our yesterdays." As a type and an exemplar of this existence we are shown one occupying our "intellectual throne" who can do no better than recount for our dubious benefit "all his store of sad experience," his "wretched days," "misery's birth," and "how the dying spark of hope was fed" (ll.181–90). In him the essentially backward, devitalized, "realistic," thinking of the contemporary intellect is personified. The state indicated is unhealthy, nerveless, and guilty of self-pity.

In contrast, the Scholar is forward-searching: his very being is creatively pointed. We, it is said, "wait like thee, but not, like thee, in hope" (l.170); and again, "none has hope like thine" (l.196). He is "nursing" his "project in unclouded joy," with no doubts (l.199). In religious phraseology, he has faith. But his faith is less intellectual than instinctive, an "impulse," and this impulse is freedom, and pushes forward:

> Still nursing the unconquerable hope,
>   Still clutching the inviolable shade,
>   With a *free onward impulse* brushing through,
>   By night, the silver'd branches of the glade.
>
> (l.211)

Because he possesses uncontaminated this expectance, his very being is orientated forward. This is the difference between his waiting and ours.

Such is the challenge which our poem levels against the intellectual and spiritual confusions of the "light half-believers" and "casual creeds" (l.172) of Arnold's day. The challenge is precise enough, since there clearly exist areas of wisdom and faculties of the mind neither tapped nor respected by the western tradition.

That tradition is symbolized by the Shepherds with whom the poem opens. These, though to be grouped with the "smock-frock'd boors" (l.59) among those who see the Scholar, are also to be understood as an adverse party—we may recall that the Scholar is repelled by the "drink and clatter" (l.61) of the inn—within the strict forms of the pastoral, and originally Greek, convention. Pastoral can carry a number of meanings, personal, poetic, academic, and religious. In "Lycidas" pastoral phrases ("drove a field," "battening our flocks") apply to Milton and King studying at Cambridge; in "the hungry sheep look up and are not fed" the implications are religious; and the river Camus and St. Peter appear together. When in "The Scholar-Gipsy" the Shepherd is told not to "leave thy wistful flock unfed" (l.3) we think inevitably of Milton, but the reference is here rather academic than religious. Our first two stanzas acknowledge the rights of the established tradition by day, but at nightfall, when the "fields are still," and men and dogs "gone to rest" (ll.6–7), we as "shepherds" are to renew the other, more mystic and mysterious, quest (l. 10). The distinction is important and applies throughout. The shepherds are creatures of day and nature cultivated; the Scholar, though in the past associated with "the sparkling Thames" (l.202), is now mainly a creature of night, and of wild nature.

The quest (i.e., to find the Scholar) is to be undertaken by night, when the "green" is "moon-blanch'd" (l.9). The Scholar himself is seen "on summer nights" crossing the Thames (l.73); his eyes rest "on the moonlit stream" (l.80); he roams through "the darkening fields" (l.84); and looks down on "the line of festal light" in Christ Church (l.129). Children see him gazing on the flocks by day, and going off "when the stars come out" (l.109); he is one to "brush" through, "by night, the silver'd branches of the glade" (l.214) and listen in woodland depths to the nightingales (l.220). The association is carried on into the corresponding figures of our similes; he is urged to "plunge deeper in the bowering wood" like Dido among the shades of Hades (ll.207–10); the Tyrian ship holds on its course by day "and night" (l.243); and the "dark Iberians" come down from "cloudy cliffs" (l.248). The Scholar's eyes were "dark" (l.99). When light and the Scholar draw close, it is at an "abandon'd" spot "where black-wing'd swallows haunt the glittering Thames" (l.94).

On the other side we have the weighty harvest, noon, and sun impressions of our first stanzas; and, since the poem is mainly about the Scholar, there is nothing more to record until the Greek ship's "emerging prow" seen at "sunrise" (l.233). Nature is here civilized. We open with "distant cries of reapers in the corn" (l.19), and, though there are wild flowers in the third stanza, they are "scarlet poppies" that "peep" through the "thick corn," convolvulus creeping "round green roots and yellowing stalks," and "lindens" that "*bower*" the poet comfortably from the sun (ll.23–29). Nature is either directly cultivated, or, in its general effect, civilized, humanized. The flocks arc part of man's civilization, as are the "feeding kine" later (l.108). The Grecian coaster of the concluding simile emerges from "*cool*-hair'd creepers" (l.234) that recall the "tendrils" and shady "air-swept lindens" earlier (ll.25–26), and is freighted with grapes, wine, figs, and tunnies (ll.238–39). Here, as in our pastoral opening, there is material abundance; but it is never quite satisfying. There is something enervate and oppressive about the heat, "scent," and "perfum'd showers" (l.27) of our early stanzas. We have noise in "nor let thy bawling fellows rack their throats" (l.4), the bleating of sheep and cries of reapers (ll.18–19), a noisy and tiring activity like the "drink and clatter" of the inn (l.61), and the "sick hurry" of our contemporary civilization so emphatic later (l.204); or, in gentler phrase, "all the live murmur of a summer's day" (l.20). The noon sun is a burning weight (l.29). So the poet craves relaxation, and takes up, for relief, the Scholar's story (l.32).

The pastoral poetry and the Greeks, with sun and cultivated nature, fall on one side; and on the other, we have the Scholar, the Gipsies, Dido, and the Tyrian trader, at home with the shadows of nighttime or the underworld, and with nature wild and untrimmed.

The Gipsies are themselves called a "wild brotherhood" (1.38). The Scholar himself haunts the "green-muffled Cumner hills" (1.69), pointing on to the dark Iberians descending from their "cloudy cliffs" (1.248); he gathers wild woodland flowers (ll.78, 86–89); is seen at a waste spot, near "breezy grass," sitting on an "o'er-grown" bank (ll.93, 97); is so much part of the forest that the feeding blackbird is not disturbed by his passing (1.116); battles with the snow on the heights (1.124); was perhaps buried under flowering nettles (1.139); plunges deep in the woods, and brushes through them by night (ll.207, 213–14). He is a creature of solitude (1.210), withdrawn from, but watching, the doings of man. He is said to "watch" (i) the "threshers" and "feeding kine" (ll.103–8), and (ii) "the line of festal light in Christ-Church hall" (ll.128–29); and these twin interests help further to establish the identity of pastoral and education. He watches like a presiding, perhaps even a guardian, spirit.

Our images of wild nature attain their climax in the Tyrian trader fleeing across the "blue," and safe, Mediterranean, past "soft" Sicily, out to "where the Atlantic raves" (ll.244–46). Nature's darkness, cold, or violence hold no terrors for Scholar or Tyrian. The Grecian ship, we may remember, was called a "coaster" (1.237); it remains close to the safe boundaries of earth. But the Tyrian is at home on the deeps and with the infinite. Both Scholar and Tyrian may, however, be afraid, or "shy" (ll.70, 79), of human contacts, except with those who deeply want, and have some right to possess, what they have to offer, as when the Scholar gives the maidens of Maytime piety his flowers (ll.82–90), or the Tyrian finds a market for his wares among the "shy" (1.249) Iberians. The Scholar himself may be supposed to fear especially the shepherds, whom he occasionally meets (1.57), but avoids, and who are always trying to catch him:

> And I myself seem half to know thy looks,
>   And put the shepherds, Wanderer, on thy trace.
>   (1.62)

He is that for which our schools of learning are always searching; which, indeed, they exist, precisely, to discover; to which the poet, who is himself "half"—but only "half"—in the Scholar's world, would direct them; but which has always found, though perhaps it need not continue to find, its chief enemy in the established schools.

Arnold's poem confronts our western tradition with suggestions of a wisdom, lore, or magic of oriental affinities or origin. The intellectual legacy of ancient Greece has clamped down with too exclusive a domination, too burning a weight of consciousness, or intellect; and the practical genius of Rome has reinforced it in the field of public affairs. Our consciousness has become, to use Nietzsche's terms, too purely "Apollonian," too heated, and needs fertilization again from the cool depths of the "Dionysian," the more darkly feminine, and eastern, powers. Both "The Scholar-Gipsy" and *The Birth of Tragedy* see our contemporary culture as too purely academic, a new Alexandrianism; materially fecund, but spiritually static, infertile, and dead. Such a criticism is not new. The mind-structure of Europe has had need, again and again, of fertilization from the older, and deeper, wisdom. So the Olympian hierarchy was challenged by the cult of Dionysus; so the developing stream of Classical culture was saved, modified, and reinforced by Christianity; so Medieval religion was challenged by Faust and by Renaissance poetry which, though it owes much to Greece, contains deep-bedded in it a mass of wisdom from the esoteric cults, and the East. But this is a process we are still within, and of which "The Scholar-Gipsy" itself is part.

The wisdom is old, and nature-rooted; and yet it is the young rather than the old who understand it. True, the Greeks were "the young, light-hearted Masters of the waves" (1.241); but here "young" drives home rather their function as the youth of a long story, with youthful confidence, and over-confidence; and we all know what has become of its maturity. The Scholar's youth is different: based on an age-old wisdom, it is yet a "perennial youth" (1.229), knowing nothing of maturity. Such is the spirit of wonder and devotion nurturing the divine spark, or *atman*, which shall eventually kindle the mind of man into powers beyond our imagining. Therefore, though a "truant" from learning, he is that learning's sole justification and final hope, as indeed the questing shepherds realize; since, in so far as academic studies become blind to the central powers, they are dead. That is why the Scholar, who rejects Oxford, becomes, through that very act of dissatisfaction and further seeking, its guardian deity.

"The Scholar-Gipsy" is a perfect example of the way in which such elusive truths as it handles should be projected through a poetic organization. They may, indeed, be truths beyond the personal thinking of the poet himself, and I leave it to others to discuss their relation to the rest of Arnold's work. But all such investigations would be no more than ancillary: the poem is what it is, and says what it says, independently of external corroboration. Its true nature and meaning can only be apprehended by attention to its various effects in mutual, and spatial, interaction; and from such an approach we gain insight into the poetry's, which is not necessarily the poet's, wisdom.

WILLIAM ROBBINS

Seed-Bed

For this and that way swings
The flux of mortal things
Though moving inly to one far-set goal.
—"Westminster Abbey"

Some of Matthew Arnold's best-known titles—*Culture and Anarchy, Literature and Dogma*, "Pagan and Medieval Religious Sentiment"—suggest opposing ideas; many of his poems convey a poignant or bitter sense of hopeless alternatives, in a life where man is either "madman or slave," or wanders "between two worlds." As distillations of his thought, from reading and experience and observation, such memorable phrases have reinforced the familiar view of the young Arnold as oscillating and vacillating, or as the prototype of the modern alienated mind. Dual, divided, dichotomized (the terms vary), he was unable as poet to resolve the conflict of the "two desires" driving him to the world without or to solitude, but his choice was foreshadowed in his farewell to Obermann, "I in the world must live." By an act of will, he settled "the dialogue of the mind with itself," turning to critical prose and the prophet's role and a qualified acceptance of the spirit of the age. An extreme version of this outcome is seen in Auden's sonnet, "Matthew Arnold." Obeying and echoing his father's voice, Arnold "thrust his gift in prison till it died," and became the elegant Jeremiah to "a gregarious optimistic generation / That saw itself already in a father's place."

These critical and psychological commonplaces, variations on a theme of inner conflict, have been persistent enough to evoke a demand for a look

From *The Arnoldian Principle of Flexibility* © 1979 by William Robbins. University of Victoria, 1979.

at other ideas in Arnold than "those revealing conflict and dualism," ideas
common to both his poetry and his prose, perhaps leading to a study of
"unity in Matthew Arnold." The conflicts are there, admittedly. Arnold's
own awareness of them is clear when he tells his sister Jane that his poems
are "fragments," like himself, "vague and indeterminate" and lacking "a
consistent meaning." The irony of his success with the modern reader in
these poems of the divided or alienated mind, in the romantic confessional
strain rather than in the classically "objective" forms of narrative and drama
that he preferred, has long been recognized. Furthermore, a number of critics
have in fact looked for a pattern of unity or consistency in Arnold's poetry
or in his writing as a whole. They have sought it in imagery, in dominant
ideas, or in pursuing even to rigorous lengths the implications in Lionel
Trilling's tribute to Arnold's "subtle critical dialectic," not always heeding
his warning that "Arnold's eclectic and dialectical method" is organic and
not mechanical, and owes its vitality to its being the method of history. Yet
a term which appears with significant frequency in Arnold's writing, and
has indeed been noted by many critics, has not had the close attention it
merits. The term is "flexibility."

The continuing emphasis on the modern relevance of Arnold's ideas
supports the judgment of H. J. Muller, that if "in an age of violence, the
attitudes he engenders cannot alone save civilization, it is worth saving chiefly
because of such attitudes." Such a tribute makes it worthwhile to decide
which of the ideas is truly fundamental. Perhaps it is better to use the word
"principle," accepting Muller's statement that Arnold's "guiding principles
remained disinterestedness, flexibility, and catholicity," and recalling Dick-
inson Miller's claim for Arnold of "a philosophy of middle principles."

The more we look into the matter, the more we incline to "flexibility"
as the basic principle, whether in its own name, or in the recurrent phrase
"a return upon oneself," or as *eutrapelia* given Attic ancestry in "A Speech
at Eton." The critical disposition of disinterestedness, the aim of "seeing the
object as in itself it really is," the harmonious balance of the four powers
making possible the civilized human being—all can be examined as in themselves key principles in Arnold's teaching. But to emphasize any of these
unduly is to risk oversimplifying or over-schematizing, to confuse insights
or formulae with principle, or to obscure the fact that Arnold's "philosophy"
combines a transcendent and absolute end (perfection) with humanistic and
relativistic means (reading and observation and experience). That perfection
as a goal cannot be attained, Arnold knows and says. To conceive of it,
however, free of doctrinal or doctrinaire rigidity, can aid man in an amoeboid
progress towards a realisable goal, "the humanisation of man in society." As

Arnold says near the end of his essay "Democracy," speaking of the need to prepare for the great social and political changes he foresaw, "Openness and flexibility of mind are at such a time the first of virtues."

This conjunction of end and means is nowhere clearer than in the Preface to the first series of *Essays in Criticism*. Alerting us to the "philosophy" that unifies this diversified body of materials, a unity more explicitly affirmed in the later preface to *Mixed Essays*, Arnold writes: "To try and approach truth on one side after another, not to strive or cry, nor to persist in pressing forward, on any one side, with violence and self-will,—it is only thus, it seems to me, that mortals may hope to gain any vision of the mysterious Goddess, whom we shall never see except in outline, but only thus even in outline." The end is truth, and the image of the mysterious Goddess implies the necessary faith and dedication as well as the unattainable end. Equal stress falls, however, on intellectual flexibility as the virtue of the true critic, on the need to avoid total commitment of a rigid or fanatical kind. In the first essay of the collection, "The Function of Criticism at the Present Time," Arnold praises Burke for his return upon himself in being able to say, after his ferocious attack on the French Revolution, that revolutionary change may sometimes be needed in human affairs. He continues with concrete example and allusion, mingling the historical and the journalistic, and prepares his reader for his summary statement on the nature of criticism.

> Criticism must maintain its independence of the practical spirit and its aims. Even with well-meant efforts of the practical spirit it must express dissatisfaction, if in the sphere of the ideal they seem impoverishing and limiting. It must not hurry on to the goal because of its practical importance. It must be patient, and know how to wait; and flexible, and know how to attach itself to things and how to withdraw from them. It must be apt to study and praise elements that for fulness of spiritual perfection are wanted, even though they belong to a power which in the practical sphere may be maleficent. It must be apt to discern the spiritual shortcomings or illusions of powers that in the practical sphere may be beneficent.

This passage is notable for the prose harmony of ideas and structure, its parallelism reinforcing the balance of practical and spiritual (or ideal); it also prepares us for the related considerations which emerge as the essay proceeds. First, the mental activity described is philosophical, in temper at least, as attaching itself to a process of growing or becoming, and as following "the ideal which is the law of its being"; secondly, this idea functions, in the famous definition, as "a disinterested endeavour to learn and propagate the best that is known and thought in the world"; thirdly, in both its nature and function criticism of this order is creative, helping us to "establish a current of fresh and true ideas," and to "nourish us in growth towards perfection." When Arnold adds that criticism as a "creative activity" must be "sincere, simple, flexible, ardent," the reminder of devotion to an ideal perfection in "sincere" and "ardent" is balanced by a reminder of the working principle in "simple" and "flexible," especially as supported by the statement that criticism must also be "ever widening its knowledge."

A careful reading of this essay makes it incredible that Arnold's "disinterestedness" should ever have been confused with indifference. It also suggests that those who have accused him of looseness and inconsistency in terminology, and when lenient excused him on grounds of strategy or situation, might in some cases at least have seen his lack of "rigour" as the sign of an adaptive and exploring mind. The development may be discursive, but it builds cumulatively on concrete particulars towards conclusions which express Arnold's meaning with precision, including the important qualification that practical efforts are suspect "if in the sphere of the ideal they seem impoverishing and limiting." Yet the essay, a watershed as his major critical manifesto, does point the semantic risk when literary criticism like Arnold's, increasingly informed by social and religious ideas, moves on to uninhibited pronouncements in all fields, in terms that often retain an element of aesthetic evalution. Beginning and ending with the literary problem of relating the creative and critical modes, the essay demonstrates the "business of the critical power" as being "in all branches of knowledge, theology, philosophy, history, art, science, to see the object as in itself it really is." Behind this expansion lay the conviction, a theme running through letters and lectures, that a world fit to write for must be a world fit to live in. Ahead lay increasing involvement in fields—social, political, religious—that the literary critic, to succeed where the poet had failed, must deal with in an effort to see life steadily and see it whole.

To disclaim expertise in these fields was not, of course, to pacify the specialist or systematic thinker detecting contradictions or inaccuracies (has Mr. Arnold, asked F. H. Bradley caustically, ever asked himself what "to verify" means?). But if taking all knowledge for his province made Arnold at times vulnerable in logic or semantics, there was compensation in being able to answer critics like Huxley on broad cultural grounds. His view of literature as being much more than *belles lettres* allowed the extension of criticism into all areas of human concern that men have written and thought about, an extension which may in itself be seen as a necessary flexibility of mind in the service of an ideal of whole and harmonious development. His seeing things as they really are is not the same objectivity as that of the man of science, though it may supply a bond or bridge; his ideal of civilized man as a balance of four powers harmonised by the "imaginative reason" lacks the logical and systematic structure of the metaphysician or the theologian. On the other hand, such a humanistic approach avoided, in his view, an incompleteness in the one and a rigidity in the other, and some lack of realism in both.

These mature formulations of 1864—the Preface to *Essays in Criticism* with the description of end and means, and "The Function of Criticism at the Present Time" listing the kinds of knowledge calling forth the critical powers—were not a breaking of new ground. The watershed metaphor used earlier reminds us that rills and springs may feed into a catchment area which in turn can send its streams through well-defined channels and sluices. Arnold may not have been the "explorer" from his earliest writings, but he had seen truth and the approach to it as multiform and manifold. Even in his poetry the anguish of the divided or alienated mind coexisted with a patient or sceptical weighing of alternatives, a resistance to premature commitment, a dislike of extremes. The man who in 1872 confessed to the "odd mixture" of Goethe, Wordsworth, Sainte-Beuve, and Newman as sources for some of his ruling ideas told his friend John Duke Coleridge as early as 1845 not to let his admiration for the sermons of Thomas Arnold change his admiration for Newman. "I should be unwilling to think that they did so in my own case, but owing to my utter want of prejudice . . . I find it perfectly possible to admire them both." The tone, half-playful, is characteristic of the young Arnold, not least in the coolly noncommittal "to admire," but the catholic and critical attitude of mind is already there, anticipating the statement in *Culture and Anarchy* that culture confronts disciples and system-makers alike with the text: "Be ye not called Rabbi!" An examination of the letters to Clough will give a glimpse of the seedbed of thinking and observation in which the principle of flexibility germinated.

Sceptical resistance to the influence of men and events did not mean indifference, as the letters and certain poems show, nor did it mean resistance to change. It was important, however, especially in revolutionary times, to distinguish between straw-fire enthusiasms for action as such, and a reasoned, informed commitment to action of a necessary and inevitable kind. The present spectacle in France, Arnold told Clough on March 1, 1848, "is a fine one," but "mostly as to the historical swift-kindling man, who is not over-haunted by the pale thought, that, after all man's shifting of posture, restat vivere." The two sonnets to Clough entitled "To a Republican Friend" express the support and the reservations soberly and fully. "God knows it, I am with you," says Arnold, in despising "The barren optimistic sophistries / Of comfortable moles," in sharing the sadness and disquiet of "earth's great ones," and in devoting "thoughts, not idle" to "the armies of the homeless and unfed." But "when I muse on what life is, I seem / Rather to patience prompted" than to hope that man, to whom Necessity leaves so narrow a margin, will see the nobler life "bursting through the network" of strife and selfishness, will see the new "day dawn at a human nod."

If it was important to be sure of right action based on right thinking, it was equally important to be sure that the action was appropriate to the actor, to his mind and talents and character. Knowing these in their true nature needed as much patience and insight as detecting the necessary direction of growth or change. To study and counsel Clough was, for Arnold, to study and counsel himself against some of his own tendencies, to observe and to escape the dangers of oscillation or paralysis. Clough could write, "It fortifies my soul to know / That though I perish, Truth is so." He could also ask bitterly whether the whole aim and purpose of our being here is to experience endless debate and frustration, and always "to fear / The premature result to draw." To avoid the "icy despair" of an Obermann in such a predicament it was futile, given Clough's clarity of vision, to make an impulsive gesture towards manning the barricades. And given the Rugby school earnestness ("I verily believe," said Clough, "my whole being is soaked through with the wishing and hoping and striving to do the school good"), there was no future in satirically realistic comment on manners and morals, a vein in which Clough was so effective, and which Arnold virtually ignored in him. With the way of Empedocles ("a devouring flame of thought") and the way of Heine ("the red fire of a sinister mockery") both unacceptable, there was only the advice of Empedocles to Pausanius ("Life still leaves human effort scope"), advice which Arnold was to take himself.

There is an increasing strain of "Don't just stand there, do something" in the letters to Clough which seems inconsistent with the earlier scepticism about "Citizen Clough" and his revolutionary zeal. The inconsistency is easily resolved. What Arnold foresaw was the disillusionment and perhaps humiliation of the idealist and intellectual rushing into the practical sphere; what he feared was the waste of a brilliant mind seeing all sides of every question so clearly that no ordinary line of action seemed worthwhile. From rallying Clough as "a mere damned depth-hunter" and "you poor subjective, you," Arnold went on to scold ("It is easier to discover what we *can* do than our vanity lets us think"); to analyze ("you are the most conscientious man I ever knew: but on some lines morbidly so"); and to prescribe (better a job with regular hours and pay, even a boring one, than the "mental harass of an uncertain life").

The "morbidly so" letter is the most revealing of the course of their friendship. Clough obviously had written at length and reproachfully, from a feeling of Arnold's growing coldness towards him. Arnold replied with reasons for his apparent neglect, including the understandable distraction of time devoted to his fiancée, making him as "egoistic and anti-social as possible." Generously taking all the blame himself, he added "I really have clung to you in spirit more than to any other man," being "for ever linked with you by intellectual bonds." Yet because Clough asked to be told where he had gone wrong, Arnold told him. Clough had completed his development, had come to his *assiette* (his true place, or foundation) before Arnold knew him. But "you were always poking and patching and cobbling at the *assiette* itself— . . . looking for this or that experience, and doubting whether you ought not to adopt this or that mode of being." By this morbid conscientiousness, "you have I am convinced lost infinite time," and spoiled "your action." It is not good, Arnold added three months later, to lay bare constantly the foundations of "individual moral constitutions," any more than to do so with the constitution of a State—not good, we may assume, for action or for friendship. It would be much better, as he had told Clough over a year earlier, before we reach the "deviceless darkness" to try at least "*some* of the things men consider desirable."

The homely and saving action urged in these letters is a far cry from the restless involvement mocked in 1848, when Arnold exaggeratedly refused to be "sucked for an hour even into the Time Stream" in which Clough and some of their friends "plunge and bellow." It was the kind of action now possible to Arnold himself, compatible with the cautious scepticism of a man "whose one natural craving is not for profound thoughts, mighty spiritual workings etc. etc. but for a distinct seeing of my own way as far as my own nature is concerned." When we add to this declaration of independence the cry to Clough, "for God's sake let us be neither fanatics nor yet chaff [*sic*] blown by the wind," we see that the most important duality in Arnold is a duality of aim or search, to understand himself and to understand the world. Both searches are philosophical in positing a reality behind appearances. The first is the theme of much of his poetry, whether the search is through Marguerite or Empedocles. The second, apparent in poems and in his letters to Clough, meant keeping aloof from the "morally worthless" excitements of the "damned times," for the sake of a clear eye and a reasoned judgment. What relates the two is the compelling need to form one's own character, yet to remain in contact with reality. Perpetual self-analysis, the sterile "dialogue of the mind with itself," would lead at best to a bleakly stoical self-sufficiency; a complete rejection of any involvement with contemporary life would mean a spiritual retreat akin to that of Obermann or the Carthusian monks.

Using Clough as an anvil to beat out his thoughts, Arnold was able to say by 1852 that "nothing can absolve us from the duty of doing all we can to keep alive our courage and our activity." The action would be of his own kind and in his own way. A life of "fluctuations" and of "new beginnings, disappointments new," he admitted to Clough, makes one "tired at last of one's own elasticity." Here is the negative term, fit metaphor for oscillation between tension and inertia. With the move into the world and "activity," it is metamorphosed over the next decade into the positive virtue of flexibility, the fruit of those preparatory years of wide reading and detached observation. Empirical in operation, the flexible principle is seen as compatible with, even as essential to, a degree of meaningful progress towards the realization of an ideal.

The persistence of this transcendental element in Arnold's thought, a belief in a "power not ourselves" giving substantive truth to our moral and spiritual values, prevents us calling him a pragmatist (a kinship neatly suggested by Trilling when he says that had William James not read Arnold we might suspect that Arnold had read William James). At the same time, his distrust of logic and rationality as adequate for interpreting man's total experience extended to a mistrust of metaphysical systems, in agreement that metaphysics calls for aid on sense. One cannot deny that inconsistent positions and contradictory statements appear in Arnold's prose criticism, any more than one could deny that conflict and polarity mark much of his verse. But the search for a realisable ideal meant accepting the need for growth and adaptability, if literary skills and literary materials were to be employed not merely as the expression of private emotion, but as a force in the service of a catholic humanism. Accepting the view of Arnold as no formal philosopher, then, we may yet, like Miller, see him as having "a philosophy of middle principles," developed by a search for wisdom through years that bring the philosophic mind. The image of the mysterious Goddess to be sought patiently along many paths, and seen then if at all only in outline, makes of flexibility both a principle and a method, distinct from our ordinary and casual use of the term for any kind of compromise. Indeed, it may be said that flexibility as a unifying principle subserves that kind of unity and consistency claimed for his work by Arnold himself in his preface to *Mixed Essays*. The "unity of tendency" the volume has in the "variety of subjects" it contains is the aim "to make civilisation pervasive and general," so that the cultivation of man's instincts and powers may give substance to the "sentiment of the ideal life."

The sense of purpose and achievement in this preface of 1879 carries us back to Arnold's comment on *Essays in Criticism* in a letter of January 21, 1865. He was "struck by the admirable riches of human nature that are brought to light in the group of persons of whom they treat, and the sort of unity that as a book to stimulate the better humanity in us the volume has." In each case unity in diversity is affirmed, with the civilising of humanity the major concern. Another letter in November, deploring the possible decline of England for want of ideas, for failure to perceive how the world is going, shows the emerging prophet of culture as his father's son in determination to prevent this decline if he can, and as his radically different self in the means and materials he will choose.

WILLIAM E. BUCKLER

Arnold and the Crisis of Classicism

Every student of Arnold is aware not only of his profound veneration of and faith in the best literature but also of his general dissatisfaction with contemporary literature as an expression of a "deeply *unpoetical*" age and his oft-repeated unfavorable comparison of the greatest Romantic writers, despite full acknowledgment of their extraordinary achievement, with the greatest writers of Classical Greece. His was a failed age creatively, Arnold thought, and the second part of his career was largely devoted to an explicit effort to establish the bases for a sound criticism that would enable the literature of the future to live fully up to such creative potential as it might have. But England had no exemplary creative writers (that is, no poets) during the 1840s, 1850s, and 1860s to whom the young writer of his generation could turn for guidance. There was more to be learned from Newman than from anyone else—habits of thought, style—but Newman was, by Arnold's terms, a supremely critical rather than a supremely creative writer.

In his prose criticism, Arnold would fault even the great Romantics for the inadequacy of their ideas (they did not know enough); for the negligent way in which they selected their poetic "actions" (their subjects or myths); and for their failure to give the action primary consideration in a poem's internal evolution, their disproportionate emphasis on phrase-making for its own sake, and their woeful inattention to the construction or architectural aspects of poems. In his poetry, on the other hand, he sketched general patterns in the disheveled psychology of an age of Romantic Modernism to

From *On the Poetry of Matthew Arnold: Essays in Critical Reconstruction.* © 1982 by New York University. New York University Press, 1982.

whose inadequacy an inadequate literature was contributive. Being an un-heroic age, it had little capacity to recognize either human protagonists of truly heroic proportions or its own desperate need of them. Being blind to its own true character and yet fixated on itself, it lacked an understanding of the austere beauty and genuine poetic relationship between the Classical ideals of full self-knowledge and complete self-effacement; thus writers be-came its mentors in ignorance of the fact that they themselves were trans-parent products of the age and bore in their own persons its disqualifying faults. The growing tendency of contemporary writers to emphasize "psy-chology and the anatomy of sentiment" contradicted the Classical recognition that the "grand[est] moral effects" of literature are "produced by *style;* thus literature's Classical capacity to treat the most complex moral themes was dissipated in formless ingenuity and capricious inflations of a poetic language whose salutary effects depend on simplicity, directness, and rapidity of movement. Moreover, its psychology of imaginative and moral development was grossly oversimplified resulting in too great a dependence on "wonders," "rapture," and "Fancy's dispossession of reality" rather than on "stern re-solve," "sterner will," sorrow, and terror, and a disposition to allow a "su-perfluity of joy," a "nectarous poppy," or stoical disdain to blind one to the deep revelation inherent in "Glooms that enhance and glorify the earth" and in the stark "majesty of grief." An age of Romantic Modernism needed, above all else, a strong current of critical thought, but instead there was a predominant allegiance to feeling, to sensuous delight in its most refined manifestations or to extremely volatile swings of passion, drawing man away from the austerer implications of thought and closer and closer to spiritual atrophy. As the craving for a life of sensation, whether of the gross or delicate sort, became systemic, as the age's demand for melodramatic fictions and apocalyptic themes became obsessive, its finer literary spirits almost de-spaired of establishing a co-creative relationship with their readers in which truly original and finely tuned aspects of poetry could continue to function processively. The therapeutic Classical process of mythmaking, of creating effective fictions that enable a person to project outward the primary images of his own inner life and to discover satisfactory patterns of resolution to life's disappointments, ran the danger of being lost.

Arnold surveyed the field of letters in this era of Romantic Modernism and identified three barometric voices as representative of literature's position in relation to man's contemporary problems: the apocalyptic voice of an intense social conscientiousness, urgent, melodramatic; the aesthetic, pastoral voice piping reassurances about "breathless glades, cheered by shy Dian's horn, / Cold-babbling springs,— or caves"; and the grim, blunt, necessitarian voice dogmatically dismissing idealistic expectations of human redemption and renewal. Implicit in this literary construct was a thoroughly distressed attitude toward man's social situation insofar as it related to literature: when brought face to face through literature with a truly horrifying human evil, neither the most poetical voice of the age nor the least poetical touched the problem in any adequate way, each being enclosed in its own intellectual and literary system and in that sense imprisoned in irrelevance. Arnold certainly knew such conspicuous exceptions to this profile as Carlyle and Tennyson, but he was somewhat alienated from them both, and he was evaluating the literary situation in representative rather than exceptional terms.

He also judged as inadequate such archetypal attitudes toward poetry as that which makes the poet suffer the agonies of those whose actions he represents (sometimes called the Romantic or, after Schiller, the Sympathetic attitude) and that which invites the poet to emulate the gods, seeing and knowing all but remaining impervious, in their untroubled happiness, to the pain which they witness (sometimes called the Olympian attitude). As Arnold saw it, such essentially pre-Classical or primitive views, though ingratiatingly naïve, ignored the moral imperative at the center of the age of the heroes, of *homo agonistes*, which simultaneously defines both literature and the human role in an entirely new way, lodging literature's function and man's identity, not in a sensual and riotous nature, but in moral values in which the gods themselves are complicit and in which empathetic understanding replaces the raw force of a soul-devouring identification through feeling.

Finally, there is the troublesome but indispensable question of literary models: to what predecessors could a young writer in such an age turn for guidance, what poets could he emulate? The question must be answered with a high degree of circumspection because, as some critics have failed to notice, nowhere in his poetry does Arnold answer it directly. Each speaker in his poetic canon is himself reacting to the pressures of Romantic Modernism, and it is not safe to assume that any two of them are the same except in poems designated by the poet as sequential, and even there the mood of the speaker and his assumption of a particular role in different but sequential poems can make a significant difference. Even the sonnet "Shakespeare" and the triple epicede "Memorial Verses" reflect very different moods of character that are explicitly generic ("We," "us") and therefore metaphoric rather than literally authorial. The result is that, however explicit the speaker's critical judgment may be, there is no firm implication of a crisp authorial judgment. Rather, criticism is angled into life, so to speak: what would a certain kind of temperament struggling with personal, if representative, crisis of consciousness *feel* about Goethe or Wordsworth or Byron or Shelley or Senancour, for example? While the resultant evaluation is impressively implanted in the reader's awareness, the relative poetic circumstances are implanted too, and the reader-critic is invited to set aside for the moment so-called objective criticism and to judge, for example, the aptness of such critical metaphors as Shelley's "lovely wail," "The pageant of [Byron's] bleeding heart," and Senancour/Obermann's ostrich-like hidden head from inside the sensibility stresses of the speaker-protagonist of "Stanzas from the Grande Chartreuse."

In the prismatic view provided by Arnold's poetry as a whole, no nineteenth-century writer escapes qualification, and only Wordsworth emerges as a model, though a profoundly challenging model, for the young writer. Coleridge never attains a poetic presence; Shelley, though treated with a fair degree of tenderness, is indicted for an ineffectual eloquence rooted in doubtful motives and for a mournful birdsong having little or no significance; despite his formalistic usefulness to Arnold himself, Keats is associated with the "nectarous poppy" of "To a Gipsy Child by the Sea-Shore" and the withdrawn, inconsequential pastoral piper of "To George Cruikshank . . ."; Senancour, even for the speaker-protagonist of "Stanzas in Memory of the Author of 'Obermann'," gradually yields place to Wordsworth in the curve of the poem's narrative consciousness. Byron's Titanism and Goethe's Olympianism place them in very different positions on the spectrum of modern poetry, neither of which is in any sense negligible. But we watch their epic-like performances—Byron's "fiery . . . strife," Goethe's uncompromising seeing eye, looking undaunted upon the apocalyptic end of a dispensation—as we might watch quintessentially different heroes at the center of any cataclysmic world-rendering, affected even beyond our capacity to understand but unable to emulate either one. Wordsworth, on the other hand, performed the magical task, essential to all ages, of returning poetry to its earliest symbol, the lyre, to its earliest practitioner, Orpheus, and to its earliest purpose, the redemption of Nature in the hearts of men—that is, the reconciliation of man to a universe that he can actually see, hear, touch, smell, taste, and love. Even in an age of Romantic Modernism, there will be embodiments of sagacity and force, if not quite Goethean sagacity or Byronic force, but these "dark days" make least likely the most essential functions of poetry—the centering of experience in the benign human emotions, the dissolution of the barriers between the harsh external appearance of things and their restorative inner reality, the attuning of the human ear to the eternal music of Nature's voice—and it is this that makes Wordsworth so incomparably important in this time of passionate grossness, myopic literalness, and spiritual deafness.

Titanism, Olympianism, Orpheanism—thus even Byron, Goethe, and Wordsworth have their analogues in Classical myth and poetry. But more explicitly, Homer, Sophocles, and Epictetus are offered as Classical correctives to Romantic Modernism. Homer is there because of the clarity of his spiritual insight, a clarity that, working through inherited myth or human "history," enabled him, though blind, to see the physiognomy of the world with such wholly dependable imaginative truth that even his physical blindness did not lead him into fancifulness and caprice. The authority of the spiritual eye is also Sophocles' chief credential: his sight/insight was so "whole" and "steady" and "even-balanced" that he never fell into the inadequacies of dullness or the misleading volatilities of passion; despite the penetration of his tragic vision, he remained "mellow" and "sweet," never falling into the deanimating, eclipsing mournfulness of a Byronic Manfred. Between these two stands Epictetus, and such company justifies our seeing his insight into the truth of the human prospect as his singular merit too. He was the philosophical spokesman for the detached, self-effacing attitude toward human experience and conduct that, in their individual fashions, Homer and Sophocles absorbed into their epics and tragedies. He was the great corrector of disproportionate human expectation, not a de-spiritualizer of man but his great equalizer, postulating a philosophy of human attitudes that would enable man, at the most dependable level, to be reconciled to the truth of his situation in his universe. Seeing "things as they in fact are," then, seeing the truth without attitudinal extravagance or rebellion, is what the mind "in these bad days" most needs, and one has to overleap, not just the greater part of Romanticism, but much of the Christian tradition in literature, to find firm foundations upon which to build mental attitudes adequate to the present and the future.

Arnold's subtle, unconscious, but profound absorption of the influence of Romantic Modernism and the close correlation between his recognition and rejection of that influence and the virtual end of his career as a poet at the age, say, of thirty-five is a tantalizing subject that defies conclusive resolution. Even if one had full and relevant external data on Arnold's thoughts and motives, a detailed account in his own hand of his recognitions and resolutions in this matter, it would still generate enough theoretical questions to keep the issue forever in solution. As it is, we have very little specific guidance for dealing with a literary event that is not only the chief critical turning in Arnold's own literary life but also the prototype of one of the major critical dilemmas of modern poetry, the difference between Arnold and his successors being that he faced it first and with incomparable *éclat*. The two fundamental questions at the heart of the event are these: what is the purpose of poetry, especially though not exclusively poetry in a modern context, and how imperative for my own poetic practice, indeed for my very continuation as a poet, is a deep and conscientious sense of poetry's purpose? Inherent therein is one of the most relentless of moral questions— *am* I what I *believe?*—and an understanding of the true dimensions of Arnold's essentially aesthetic "action" requires a moral context.

The two documents that Arnold himself placed at the center of the issue are *Empedocles on Etna* and the critical Preface of 1853, the one "A DRA- MATIC POEM" Classically monitored and Romantically faulted, the other a poetic manifesto subscribing unequivocally to the dramatic principles of Classical theory and practice and faulting Romanticism for its deviations from those principles. Such central placement is perfectly apt—these are the crucial exemplary documents—but something more than a literal view of them, in fact a metaphoric or symbolic view, must be taken in order to appreciate fully their subtle, oblique significance. *Empedocles on Etna* was Arnold's Iphigenia, the symbolic sacrifice that he made to appease the wrath of the goddess of pure poetry for an offense that, though innocently com- mitted, had become systemic in his practice of her art. The Preface of 1853, besides being an explicit declaration of full faith in the simple, austere, unimpeachable poetic rules of the Classical goddess, is an implicit confession of personal culpability, a plea of "guilty, with an explanation."

The issue is not whether or not Arnold was right in thus indicting the major tendency of his poetic art: that is a legitimate but different issue upon which much critical impressionism has been expended. Here our concern is simply with how he saw the matter, and since the Preface is the chief summary of evidence external to the poetry, the Preface is the place to begin.

Throughout Arnold's Preface, aesthetics is rooted in ethics: that is good poetry which increases the world's pleasure, that is bad poetry which in- creases the world's pain is how the Preface begins. It ends with a fingering of culture's amoralists, poetry's *dilettanti,* and a solemn moral charge to its writer-audience: "Let us not bewilder our successors: let us transmit to them the practice of poetry, with its boundaries and wholesome regulative laws, under which excellent works may again, perhaps, at some future time, be produced, not yet fallen into oblivion through our neglect, not yet condemned and cancelled by the influence of their eternal enemy, caprice." Thus it is an action Preface, a call to self-recognition and self-renewal or self-restraint, in the light of a refreshed view of the highest kind of moral seriousness involved in the practice of poetry, and a challenge even to accept what for the writer is the ultimate self-sacrificial insight, namely, that an age of no poetry is better than an age of bad poetry. That "human actions" are the "eternal objects" of poetry makes it axiomatic that aesthetic considerations, however indispensable, are secondary to the moral imperative; even the selections of "an excellent action"—one which "belong[s] to the domain of our permanent passions"—invokes, in the first place, a high degree of moral sophistication, though it is at this point that ethics and aesthetics merge and become inseparable as poetic functions, moral affect being thereafter dependent on style. But even such stylistic matters as construction and diction are dealt with in the language of morality, the rhetoric of conscience: the "severe and scrupulous self-restraint of the ancients" in these matters has, for those who have commerce with them, "a steadying and composing effect upon their judgment, not of literary works only, but of men and events in general."

So pervasive in the Preface that it determines its structure is the contrast between the ancients and the moderns, between the Classical Greeks and Romantic Modernist Englishmen. Against the illusion exuded by "the great monuments of early Greek genius"—"the calm, the cheerfulness, the disinterested objectivity"—is set the frenzied chaos of contemporary English poetic practice, with its fragmentariness of view and of performance, its preference for the rhetorical over the genuinely poetical, for the novel and curious part over the impressive and salutary whole, its subjectivity, its inflated contemporaneity, its overabundance of critical counselors, its spiritual confusion, incoherence, and discomfort inducing feelings of contradiction, irritation, and impatience, its lack of moral grandeur, its excessive self-congratulation, its "bewildering confusion" and uncertainty in all respects, the imperious demands it makes for devotion to such provincially topical subjects as theories of progress, industrial development, and social amelioration, its blind expectation that a poetry can be true to the best poetic principles and at the same time faithfully represent so fundamentally unpoetical an age.

And here is where we identify the implicit confession of personal culpability: although Arnold acknowledged at the time of writing the Preface that a poetry that took as its essential object the representation of such an age as that described above could hardly be anything but poetically inadequate because its subject was woefully inadequate and no craftsmanship, however expert, could make adequate poetry out of an inadequate subject, he had largely done just that. It is true that he had consistently represented the age in order to subject it and the Romantic writers who had fathered it to relentless criticism; one may easily yield him credit for having done something far more poetically imaginative than simply creating verse structures through which his persistent critical consciousness could function at a subtle and highly stimulating level. But on the whole and despite notable exceptions, the dominant impression that Arnold's poetry gives to one who knows something of his age is of a representation of that age.

Arnold rooted the feeling of his poems and the rhetoric expressive of that feeling in the Classical tradition of mimetic, representational art, his lyrical as well as his dramatic and narrative poems having, despite their confessional mode, the essential objectivity of action-centered poetry that is "in a large degree dramatic or personative in conception." That he lacked the "discipline" to do it plainly and simply and thoroughly, he confesses, and he admits that therefore his poems do not "breathe its spirit" but he still claims, even in the face of confessed failure, that throughout his career as a young poet he had, in an immature, undisciplined, unsuccessful way, aspired to the goal of the ancients—"not to praise their age, but to afford to the men who live in it the highest pleasure which they are capable of feeling." Judged by the severe standards of the Preface, he had been prone to three basic types of error: of allowing too many relatively inconsequential pieces a place among his published works; not only of critically interpreting his age, but of interpreting it in such a way as to make too many of his poems time-dependent; of grossly miscalculating what gives readers of poetry "the highest pleasure which they are capable of feeling." He had succeeded in catching "the main movement of mind of the last quarter of a century," "the main line of modern development"; he had been more attentive than any of his contemporaries before Swinburne to the relevance of Classical style to a modern outlook, to the wholesome persistence in an unpoetical age of a supremely poetical tradition. He had put in place, however unsatisfactorily from his own point of view, a canon of poetry that, though it is the least revolutionary in appearance, has had a profound relevance for modern poetry. As Arnold was both the most Wordsworthian and Classical of Victorian poets, so Hardy and Eliot have been the most Arnoldian and Classical of twentieth-century poets.

Clearly, then, Arnold did not need to go on simply doing more of the same, especially in the face of the firmest possible declaration of the purpose and guiding principles of poetry that was at the same time an implicit confession of the inadequacy of his own poetic practice. He was not a dilettante according to Goethe's strict definitions cited in the final paragraph of the Preface, but it would have been dilettantish to go on producing confessedly inadequate poems. There is an unmistakable and decisive self-reference in the following perorative sentence: "If we must be *dilettanti:* if it is impossible for us, under the circumstances amidst which we live, to think clearly, to feel nobly, and to delineate firmly: if we cannot attain to the mastery of the great artists—let us, at least, have so much respect for our art to prefer it to ourselves." It is a moral principle leading, for a thoroughly honest man, to a moral decision: better no poetry at all than more of the same inadequate poetry.

Arnold had specifically claimed for *Empedocles on Etna* the literary virtue of firm delineation, and it is perhaps easiest to credit Arnold's poems generally with that quality, including the poems or conceptions of poems that Arnold would have had to fault by other standards. So it seems most profitable to look elsewhere for *the reason for the fault* of *Empedocles on Etna* and the other poems for which it was a symbolic sacrificial stand-in, such poems, for example, as "Stanzas in Memory of the Author of 'Obermann',", "Tristram and Iseult," "The Scholar-Gipsy," and "Stanzas from the Grande Chartreuse." Arnold designates the fault quite explicitly—a spiritually devastating pathos rather than a tragedy that becomes spiritually restorative through the credible conversion of human catastrophe into human admiration and delight. But the really teasing question is how a poet so Classically oriented as Arnold and so persistently critical of Romantic Modernism as we have seen him to be could have fallen or drifted into a position so untenable for one like him—in short, *the reason for the fault*.

In the first place, we should note that the fault was not poetically inherent in the "historical" account of Empedocles—historically inherent, perhaps, but not poetically inherent. Arnold specifically says that the error was a literary one—"as I have endeavoured to represent him." This points to one reason for an error in judgment: Arnold was so fascinated by the historical Empedocles that he very carefully portrayed the historical Empedocles, unmindful for the moment of something that he knew very well, namely, Aristotle's distinction between historical responsibility and a higher poetic responsibility: "The true difference is that one relates what has happened, the other what may happen. Poetry, therefore, is more philosophical and a higher thing than history: for poetry tends to express the universal, history the particular." Further, Arnold describes his discovery of Empedocles in terms that suggest why he was led into a disproportionate emphasis on history: "Into the feelings of a man so situated there entered much that we are accustomed to consider as exclusively modern." That was itself a lesson that might be well taught to his chauvinistic contemporaries; and, along with certain other tendencies of his overtly pedagogical temperament, this led Arnold to teach a truth somewhat lower than the highest poetical truth to which his subject was susceptible.

This failure of the poet to interfere with history in the name of poetry's higher purpose is also characteristic of the other poems cited above: relentless fidelity to character and imagined circumstance brings them to the end of a linear progression for which there is no compensatory reversal and recognition, no establishment of a sternly reassuring alternative possibility (the "what may happen" of poetry versus the "what has happened" of history).

No imaginative salvation is made available to any of the protagonists. The chilling last line of "Tristram and Iseult" suffuses the whole literary experience with a hint of spiritual bitterness; the coda of "The Scholar-Gipsy" darkens the future prospect into a suggestion of futility and ultimate failure; the speaker-protagonists of "Stanzas in Memory of the Author of 'Obermann' " and "Stanzas from the Grande Chartreuse" are victims of a temperamental malaise, the one engaged in an endless search for the very "dreams" that his sceptical nature rejects, the other in a myth of no return.

Why? Because Arnold the poet, despite his persistent critical insights, had become to a significant degree the victim of the very modern history, the Romantic Modernism, that he delineated so firmly and so well. That there should be this discrepancy between his principles and his practice shows that, "under the circumstances in which [he] live[d]," he could not "think clearly" at that imaginative level of thinking that holds poetry true to the poet's principles. Though he could articulate a resounding defense of the modern hero—an Odysseus-like figure who accepts the "general law" of the universe as it in fact is, sees "one clue to life, and follow[s] it," and, "Laborious, persevering, serious, firm," pursues his "track, across the fretful foam / Of vehement actions without scope or term, / Called history . . . "— he so suffered from his era's despair of modern heroism that he devoted his poetic talent and energy to the creation of human types who had ceased to "feel nobly" except in vastly diminished remnant terms and declined the responsibility of the poet-in-charge to give their myths an ennobling turn. Thus the critic of Romantic Modernism had himself become a Romantic Modernist. When Arnold recognized this, he made the most critical decision a poet who venerates his art can make—to correct it even at the cost of ceasing to be a poet altogether.

Despite an essentially detached and good-humored record, it is difficult to imagine that Arnold underwent this crisis in his literary life without some degree of Sturm und Drang. It may not have been an event as traumatizing as Carlyle's detection and defiance of the Devil or Mill's irrepressible "No!" to happiness or Newman's discovery of the face of a heretic in his Monophysite mirror or Tennyson's sudden loss of the chief support of his imaginative and emotional life, but it is reminiscent of them all. It was certainly more severe an act of moral/aesthetic self-measuring than most gifted young poets ever subject themselves to, and the results were about as far-reaching as possible, altering the whole course of Arnold's literary life. But Arnold kept his own counsel with Classical aplomb. He was not himself subject to the demonic self-consciousness that possessed some of his contemporaries and some of his own imaginary characters, and even his most confessional

moments show an admirable restraint. Modern life was a most serious business, and modern poetry was modern man's chief instrument of articulation
and reconciliation. He had, for a substantial period of time, offered it his
dedicated service, but as the task became more and more demanding, the
need more and more urgent, he recognized with exemplary honesty and
without the least suggestion of false modesty his own poetic limitations. His
contribution had been substantial, and though he had a genuine if limited
faith in its ultimate serviceability, he saw no need to go on replicating it.
Instead, he undertook the difficult and delicate task of writing a brief but
full-bodied declaration of poetic faith and an oblique confession of poetic
inadequacy. It was a very courageous and forthright action for a young man
who had thus far appeared before the reading public only as "A." As literary
history would have it, both the difficulty and the delicacy were richly re-
warded: in the whole century, Arnold's Preface of 1853 is surpassed in
importance only by Wordsworth's Preface to the Second Edition of *Lyrical
Ballads*. With it, Arnold launched the most spectacular critical career in the
history of English letters.

Arnold and God

"Milton's power of style . . . has for its great character *elevation;* and Milton's elevation clearly comes, in the main, from a moral quality in him— his pureness. 'By pureness, by kindness!' says St. Paul. These two, pureness and kindness, are, in very truth, the two signal Christian virtues, the two mighty wings of Christianity, with which it winnowed and renewed, and still winnows and renews, the world." This is, so far as I know, Arnold's own figure, and it is the work of a poet. It borrows a little of the grotesqueness of the Old Testament cherubim and seraphim, and at the same time it calls to mind the "metaphysical" figures of those English poets who wrote in the age of "Rational Theology." It can stand as a sort of "emblem" in the seventeenth-century manner over the rest of Arnold's career as literary critic, coming as it does in his essay on Edmond Scherer, "A French Critic on Milton," which sets the perspective of this later phase of his criticism.

It is hard for the English to detach themselves from the old Puritan issue in Milton studies, and so we do well to look to a foreign critic, says Arnold, for disinterestedness; and in Scherer the French critic we have, moreover, a great "firmness and sureness of judgment." He recognizes Scherer's historical method as reaching out toward a responsible criticism, but now he finds that the historical method, "the old story of the man and the milieu," one of the basic ideas of "The Function of Criticism at the Present Time," is not altogether sufficient. "It is a perilous doctrine" that this historical method will yield of itself the right judgment or evaluation. The

From *Arnold and God.* © 1983 by the Regents of the University of California. The University of California Press, 1983.

curious case of *Paradise Lost* sets a problem for critics because the poem
depends on a theological thesis that is absurd, and hence, as Scherer says,
it is in a sense "false," "grotesque," "tiresome." But Scherer recognizes
Paradise Lost, nevertheless, as "immortal," for the great passages that are part
of the "poetical patrimony of the human race," for the incomparable lines,
the incomparable imagery, and finally above all the sustained level of *style*.
But this is not quite all, for Arnold. The style itself comes from a moral
quality. Kindness, or charity, is not one of Milton's signal virtues, but
pureness, or chastity, *is*, as Arnold's splendid citation from "Smectymnuus"
reminds us. This essay on Milton presents the Arnoldian principle that has
been formed by his writings on dogma, on God, and on the Bible, the
principle that literary criticism must ultimately take account of morals, which
is the domain of religion. Just as all Arnold's early literary criticism contributed to the shaping of his religious thought, so does now the religious
thought go to shape and direct the literary criticism.

I should like . . . to review a few of the later essays in which the
"religious" element is conspicuous, ranging from the comparativist interest
of "A Persian Passion Play" to the great influence of his youth in "George
Sand," the social-educational concern of "Literature and Science," the social-
ecclesiastical concern of "A Comment on Christmas," his old love of the
mystics in "A Friend of God," to new interests in "Amiel" and "Tolstoi."

"A Persian Passion Play" (1871) is a rather daring piece of education.
The Oberammergau Passion Play had been revived in 1871 and was much
talked of, and for Arnold to take up the celebration of the martyrdom of
Hassan and Hussein and call it a "Passion Play" is very comparative indeed.
Arnold alleges that the increasing tolerance of Protestants for Roman Cath-
olics is part of "the spread of larger conceptions of religion, of man, and of
history, than were current formerly," and this essay will appeal to that larger
interest in religion. He recounts the history of the split of Islam into the
Shiah and the Suni sects, and with quotations from Gibbon recounts the
martyrdom at Kerbela of Hassan and Hussein, the grandsons of Mahomet,
which is celebrated by the Shiite Moslems. The self-flagellation that accompanies the season of the dramas, Arnold relates back to ancient practices "on
this old Asiatic soil, where beliefs and usages are heaped layer upon layer
and ruin upon ruin," back to the priests of Baal cutting themselves with
knives. His description of the dramas, thanks in part to Gobineau, is vivid,
pathetic, and compelling. But where Gobineau ascribes the appeal of the
plays to patriotism, Arnold ascribes it to the way they answer, as Christianity
does, to "the urgent wants of human nature." He tells how when Jaffer,
Mahomet's cousin, took refuge among the Christian Abyssians and described

his religion there, the Abyssian king found that in all essentials it was like Christianity—not a straw's difference. Arnold sees more than a straw: he declares the Bible is superior to the Koran, and Christianity superior to Islam, but nevertheless, he says, these martyrdom plays do acclaim the very same "mildness and self-sacrifice" that was being celebrated at Oberammergau. In fact, Islam itself in acclaiming these virtues does in a way witness the excellence of Jesus who embodies them supremely. This last rather spoils the disinterestedness of the essay, as much as to say that if *even* this inferior religion has a place for mildness and self-sacrifice, how much better must be the religion to which they are central! And Arnold writes as though Christianity were later, more *developed* than Islam, when of course Islam arose late as a kind of reformation of the Judaeo-Christian line. But if the essay is a little weak as comparative religion, it is very strong in vividness and sympathy. The fact that events of our own time have made it particularly interesting and informative witnesses the Arnoldian ideal of cultural breadth and transmission.

The "George Sand" essay (1877) looks back on what had been a passionate interest of his youth, and in explaining her power explains his own development. Her "principal elements" are: "the cry of agony and revolt, the trust in nature and beauty, the aspiration towards a purged and renewed human society." With Arnold, the "cry of agony and revolt" had given way to the philosophical Aurelian melancholy of his poems, but otherwise his characterization of George Sand is a characterization of himself. Like him, she had early freed herself by rejecting the orthodox, literal, anthropomorphic God, "made in our image, silly and malicious, vain and puerile, irritable or tender, after our fashion." She wrote:

> It is an addition to our stock of light, this detachment from the idolatrous conception of religion. It is no loss of the religious sense, as the persisters in idolatry maintain. It is quite the contrary, it is a restitution of allegiance to the true Divinity. It is a step made in the direction of this Divinity, it is an abjuration of the dogmas which did him dishonour.
>
> (*Collected Prose Works*, ed. R.H. Super, 8:228–29, 438n.)

George Sand's vague phrase "Divine sense," Arnold says, stands for "all the best thoughts and best actions of life, suffering endured, duty achieved, whatever purifies our existence, whatever vivifies our love." Because Madame Sand is a Frenchwoman, that is to say odd, un-English, and peculiar—says the smiling Arnold—"her religion is therefore, as we might expect, with peculiar fervency social." As he goes on to play with this peculiar French and foreign idea, we know of course that it has become in Matthew Arnold an English idea, and it runs through all his work.

George Sand is quoted in the essay "Equality" (1878): "The human ideal, as well as the social ideal, is to achieve equality." If the earlier "Democracy" (1861) had not made Arnold's political views abundantly clear, "Equality" must, altogether unequivocally and consistently with his whole career. "When we talk of man's advance towards his full humanity, we think of an advance, not along one line only, but several"; *Bildung*-Culture is the way of the advance, and it is an advance for all. Humanity—Herder's *Humanität*—is marked by its recognition of every human being as an aggregation of infinite possibilities, and it is for Arnold as for Herder the inevitable and best corollary of the Christian doctrine of the uniqueness and value of the individual.

"Literature and Science" (1882) is much anthologized and much loved for its enduring defense of humane letters, even the study of Greed—even now! The education consisting of natural science, which Thomas Huxley was advocating, "leaves one important thing out of . . . account: the constitution of human nature." And human nature has an imperious need to satisfy "the sense for conduct, the sense for beauty"; what speaks to this need is something bigger than mere religion. He starts with Plato on education, "those studies which result in [man's] soul getting soberness, righteousness and wisdom," not a bad idea of education, he says, whether you are going into the House of Lords or the pork trade in Chicago. And he continues to draw on Greek literature for examples of the broadest and most humane culture, still the best to help us relate the new discoveries of science to the rest of our lives—"So strong . . . is the demand of religion and poetry to have their share in a man, to associate themselves with his knowing, and to relieve and rejoice it." The standard idea of Arnold, made all too current by T. S. Eliot, is that he proposed to substitute culture for religion—and that idea was anathema to T. S. Eliot. Arnold's idea rightly understood would still be anathema to T. S. Eliot, but it is by no means a simple idea of exchange. In this essay, medieval education and the Church that controlled it, both held up to scorn by Huxley, are presented by Arnold as a sort of temporary substitute for culture, the broad humane culture as the Greeks understood it. It was a legitimate substitute because while it neglected both humane letters and science it answered to that imperious "sense for conduct, the sense for beauty." And now "the importance of humane letters in a man's training becomes not less, but greater, in proportion to the success of modern science in extirpating what it calls 'mediaeval thinking.' " Arnold sees science as part of culture, and literary criticism as partaking of science, and right here he brings science to literature in the experimental mode, with an exhibit in the line of the paired statements of *Literature and Dogma*. Again, the heart of the matter appears to be metaphor. Compare, he says, the maxim "Patience is a virtue" with Homer: "For an enduring heart have the destinies appointed to the children of men." The maxim is all very well, but does nothing for us. But when we suffer, or are disoriented, or are emotionally bereft by some prodigious advance of modern thought, we might be advantaged by calling Homer's line to mind. Arnold tactfully leaves it unexplicated, but in the interests of a scientific criticism we might imagine its function. In the figure "the children of men" we sense the long continuity of human experience and feel a sustaining solidarity; in the "destinies" we recognize the three dark sisters as an acknowledged personification of the force-not-ourselves, and we do not have to stop to ask whether we "believe" in them or not as we might with some Christian text; personified, they can be imagined as "appointing" us certain tremendous emotional powers of endurance, *because*, we can all too easily infer, there may be so very much to endure. We know we are not evading with some sentimentality the sadness of our human lot, and we can feel therefore the satisfaction of courage, and a kind of decorum in things. And so Arnold can conclude that the " 'hairy quadruped furnished with a tail and pointed ears, probably arboreal in his habits,' this good fellow carried hidden in his nature, apparently, something destined to develop into a necessity for humane letters. Nay, more; we seem finally to be even led to the further conclusion that our hairy ancestor carried in his nature, also, a necessity for Greek."

"A Comment on Christmas" (1885) reviews the theory of miracle as symbol or figure; this time Arnold recounts the legend of the miraculous birth of Plato (ever implying that Christianity is not unique), taking it as a symbol of Plato's purity. But Plato did not found a religion and so the legend died. Jesus founded a religion (and Paul established it), and so the legend of virgin birth remained functional, and functions still as a symbol of the idea of purity—this is what we celebrate at Christmas. Lent, with the legend of the miracle of the temptation, celebrates the idea of self-conquest and self-control; Whitsuntide, with the miracle of the tongues of fire, celebrates the idea of inspiration. The two greatest ideas of Christianity are pureness and charity: France is now rather weak on purity (in her worship of the great goddess "Lubricity"), England is weak in charity. Even the Church of England has been associated too much with station and property and forgets that "Blessed are the poor in spirit," which is interpreted to mean blessed are those who are indifferent to riches. This point leads Arnold directly into the interpretation of the Christian virtue of charity as an obligation to extend economic equality: "It shall be required *of this generation.*" R. H. Super connects this essay with Arnold's "Lay Sermon" (1884) celebrating the "saints" of the Anglican Church who gave themselves to social work in London's East End. Both confirm once more Arnold's faithfulness to his father's ideal of the Broad activist Church, working toward the Kingdom of God on earth.

The essay "A Friend of God" was written as a service for a friend but represents a real interest of Arnold's—the mystic Tauler, who was associated with the fourteenth-century Swiss mystical sect, the *Gottesfreunde*, "Friends of God"; their name they took from the biblical epithet for Abraham, "the friend of God." Arnold had known Tauler early in a French version as the *Note-Books* show; in the later *Note-Books* and in this essay he quotes the English translation by his friend Morell:

> Sin killeth nature, but nature is abhorrent of death; therefore sin
> is against nature, therefore sinners can never have a joy.
>   (*Collected Prose Works*, 11:181, *The Note-Books of Matthew*
>   *Arnold*, ed. H. F. Lowry, Karl Young, and W. H. Dunn)

and acclaims the "natural truth" of such statements. He deplores the recent "crude and turbid" recrudescence of mythology in the spectacle of the Salvation Army, but insists nevertheless that even the common people are rejecting the mythological and irrational in religion, and this change creates a situation favorable to the true "Friends of God"—the Latitude Men, Butler, Wilson—Wilson whose glory Arnold says is his living and abiding sense that "sin is against nature"—and he was "the most exemplary of Anglican Churchmen." The change is favorable likewise to the mystics, "whom their heart prompted to rest religion on natural truth rather than on mythology." Jesus' words, "How hardly shall they that have riches enter into the kingdom of heaven," are interpreted by narrow literalists to mean, "If you trust in riches . . . you cannot enter after death into the paradise above the sky." But "our mystic" understood the words rightly (demythologizing): "How hardly shall they that have riches follow me and my life, live naturally, be happy."

Arnold continued through his life to practice the doctrine of *Bildung;* he continued, we know by his reading lists, to read regularly in "the best," and he continued to develop himself and turn to new ideas, new writers. The *Note-Books* reveal in some touching excerpts his determination not to yield up *Bildung* to old age; he quotes Sainte-Beuve on the Swiss moralist Charles-Victor de Bonstetten:

Cette vigilance du dedans, cette éducation continuelle . . . fait qu'on ne se fige pas à un certain âge, qu'on ne se rouille pas, et que de toute la force de son espirit on repousse le *poids* des ans.

(*Note-Books* 460)

This inward vigilance, this continual education keeps him from congealing at a certain age, from rusting, so that with all the force of his spirit he spurns the *weight* of years. [Arnold's emphasis]

He also transcribes Bonstetten's own words:

Ce n'est pas parce qu'on est jeune que l'on apprend quelque chose, mais parce que dans la jeunesse on vous tient au travail et qu'on vous fait suivre avec méthode une pensée. Dites-vous que votre inapplication et l'irrégularité ou la nullité sont la véritable cause de la stagnation de vos idées, que vous attribuez faussement à l'âge.

(*Note-Books* 485)

It is not because one is young that one learns, but because in youth one is held to work and made to follow out a thought with method. Tell yourself that your inapplication, irregularity, and vacancy are the true cause of the stagnation of your ideas, which you falsely attribute to age.

"Bonstetten died at 86," Arnold adds to the entry. And then there is a motto from Goethe frequent in the *Note-Books* from 1877 on:

Das Hervorbringen selbst ein Vergnügen und sein eigner Lohn ist.

(*Note-Books* 286 et passim)

Creation is a gratification in itself and is its own reward.

Hervorbringen (creation) is surely to be understood as Carlyle understood it and translated it: Produce! Produce!

The essay "Amiel" makes reference to this discipline. He had rejected Henri-Frédéric Amiel for some time as less than "tonic" and at first explains that he will still reject his poetry as a sort of inferior "Obermann" and will reject the speculative philosophy of the *Journals* as a bedazzled and futile Buddhism that led Amiel in fact to incapacity, to his acknowledged "increasing isolation, inward disappointment, enduring regrets, a melancholy neither to be consoled nor confessed, a mournful old age, a death in the

desert." Amiel refused to seek out the ideas that combat the paralysis of
indeterminacy: "The ideas to live with . . . are ideas staunchly counteracting
and reducing the power of the infinite and indeterminate." But Arnold finds
nevertheless that Amiel's *Journals* are admirable when he turns specific and
critical, when he does perhaps manage that discipline of creative thought.
No doubt he won Arnold by his appreciation of the office of critic. Arnold
quotes:

> Like Plato's sage, it is only at fifty that the critic is risen to the
> true height of his literary priesthood, or, to put it less pompously,
> of his social function.
>
> (11:274)

He appreciates Amiel's comparativist insight, quoting him:

> Learning and even thought are not everything. A little *esprit*,
> point, vivacity, imagination, grace, would do no harm . . . The
> Germans heap the faggots for the pile, the French bring the fire.
>
> (11:278)

And he is much interested in Amiel's sense of the social necessity for religion
and his rejection of orthodox Christianity.

> The whole Semitic dramaturgy has come to seem to me a work
> of the imagination. . . . The apologetics of Pascal, Leibnitz, Se-
> crétan appear to me no more convincing than those of the Middle
> Age, for they assume that which is in question—a revealed doc-
> trine, a definite and unchangeable Christianity. Pious fiction is
> still fiction. Truth has superior rights.
>
> (11:280–81)

With such critical insights, it is doubly to be lamented that Amiel failed in
discipline. Arnold writes:

> Toils and limits composition indeed has; yet all composition is a
> kind of creation, creation gives . . . pleasure, and, when suc-
> cessful and sustained, more than pleasure, joy. . . . Sainte-Beuve's
> motto, as Amiel himself notices, was that of the Emperor Severus:
> *Laboremus.* "Work," Sainte-Beuve confesses to a friend, "is my
> sore burden, but it is also my great resource."
>
> (11:276)

I think in this passage we find an element of Arnold's autobiography.

It is a pretty irony of history that Arnold records in a letter to his mother of 1861: he thanks her for forwarding mail including "a note returning a letter (of no importance) of a Russian count who had been sent with a letter to me." Count Leo Tolstoi was in England in 1861, particularly interested in visiting the schools, and had been recommended to the attention of Inspector Matthew Arnold. The letter "of no importance" seems important now, and one yearns to know if there was any personal exchange between Arnold and Tolstoi. There was exchange later, by way of books. Tolstoi greatly admired "The Function of Criticism at the Present Time," and then: "Tolstoi," records a memoirist,

> speaks with great praise of the religious books of Matthew Arnold. According to his words, there is an established opinion that the first place in the works of Matthew Arnold is occupied by poetry, the second by critical works, the third by religious works. It would be more correct, however, to arrange everything in reverse order. The religious works of Arnold are the best and most significant part of his works.

Ernest J. Simmons records that in 1884 Tolstoi was urging his friends to read *Literature and Dogma*, "a remarkable production" that, he said, contained many of his own thoughts. Arnold "will bring you great satisfaction because he particularly insists on destroying the notion of God as something outside us, a 'magnified man' as he calls him." And he had had his friend Chertkov present Arnold in England with a French translation of *What I Believe*. He was much taken with Arnold's "sweet reasonableness" as a term for the Christian principle he wanted to exercise in his own (much tried) family. And in 1890–91 we find him rereading *Literature and Dogma*, a "favorite" work.

Arnold, in his turn, was in some degree aware of Tolstoi since 1861; in 1887 he was reading *Anna Karénine, Ma Religion* (What I Believe), *Que Faire?* and *Ma Confession*, all in French.

Partisans of the novel as genre may take umbrage at Arnold's critical neglect of it—except for the case of George Sand. But he read novels: the *Note-Book* reading lists and *Letters* reveal a wide-ranging and pretty steady novel habit: Fielding, Sterne, Goldsmith, Austen, Scott (a positive flurry of rereading in 1873), Bulwer, Charlotte Brontë, Dickens, Thackeray, George Eliot, Trollope, Kingsley, Disraeli, Collins, Hawthorne, Stowe, Cooper, Howells, Bret Harte, George Sand (early, late, and widely), Hugo, Stendhal, Daudet, Balzac, Flaubert, Zola, Turgenev, and, before the end, Stevenson, Hardy, and James. The partisans of the novel may forgive him all critical neglect at last for the sake of his important and perspicacious essay "Count

Leo Tolstoi" (1887), which really marks the beginning of Tolstoi's reputation
in England. He explains in a letter: "I had a special reason for writing about
Tolstoi, because of his religious ideas; in general I do not write about the
literary performances of living contemporaries or contemporaries only recently dead."

He begins by greeting the genre with Sainte-Beuve's observation: the
age of George Sand and the "lyric, ideal" novel is over; now in Flaubert's
Madame Bovary we have the novel of "severe and pitiless truth." The great
English novelists are gone, Arnold says (Thackeray died in 1863, Dickens
in 1870, George Eliot 1880, Trollope 1882), the French novel has lost ground,
and it is now the Russian novel that becomes preeminent. The Russian
nature "seems marked by an extreme sensitiveness, a consciousness most
quick and acute for what the man's self is experiencing, and also for what
others in contact with him are thinking and feeling." He turns to Tolstoi,
but not to *War and Peace*, for "in the novel one prefers, I think, to have the
novelist dealing with the life he knows from having lived it." *Vanity Fair* is
to be preferred to *The Virginians*, *Anna Karénine* to *War and Peace*. *Anna
Karénine* has too many characters, too many incidents, for artistic unity, but
it is not to be taken as a "work of art" but rather as a "piece of life." He *sees*
and *lives with* Anna, Karénine, Stiva, Dolly, and the rest. He recounts how
Levine at last marries Kitty and they are profoundly happy—"Well, and
who could help being happy with Kitty? So I find myself adding
impatiently."

And the truth is, Arnold loves Anna. And this love makes something
of a problem for him. We English are a nation "qui sait se gêner," who know
how to control ourselves. "Perhaps in the Slav nature this valuable faculty
is somewhat wanting"; even in English high society there may be some laxity.

> But in general an English mind will be startled by Anna's suf-
> fering herself to be so overwhelmed and irretrievably carried away
> by her passion, by her almost at once regarding it, apparently,
> as something which it was hopeless to fight against. . . . It is the
> triumph of Anna's charm that it remains paramount for us never-
> theless; that throughout her course, with its failures, errors, and
> miseries, still the impression of her large, fresh, rich, generous,
> delightful nature, never leaves us—keeps our sympathy, keeps
> even, I had almost said, our respect.
>
> (11:289–90)

This does not create much of a critical problem for us now; it is interesting
that, for Arnold, it did, and he must work it out. The solution is that Tolstoi

never caters to the French goddess "Lubricity," as Flaubert does, whose Emma Bovary follows a course similar to Anna's. Such catering, Arnold says, as Burns said of promiscuity, *petrifies feeling*. And *Madame Bovary* is a work of *petrified feeling*. "The treasures of compassion, tenderness, insight . . . are wanting to Flaubert. He is cruel."

In recounting Levine's conversion, as Arnold says, Tolstoi had recounted his own; Levine avows at the end of the novel: he will probably continue to be imperfect,

> but my inner life has won its liberty; it will no longer be at the mercy of events, and every minute of my existence will have a meaning sure and profound which it will be in my power to impress on every single one of my actions, that of *being good*.
>
> (11:295)

Since finishing the novel, Tolstoi has gone on to write more autobiography, recounting his religious experience in more detail.

> The idea of *life* is his master idea. . . . Moral life is the gift of God, is God, and this true life, this union with God to which we aspire, we reach through Jesus. . . . This doctrine is proved true for us by the life in God, to be acquired through Jesus, being what our nature feels after and moves to, by the warning of misery if we are severed from it, the sanction of happiness if we find it. . . . Sound and saving doctrine, in my opinion, this is.
>
> (11:297)

But it might have been gathered, says Arnold, from the novel. Tolstoi, though, has gone on to work out for himself what he calls "the positive doctrine of Jesus," a scheme of five new "commandments" to replace the decalogue, which five, if all were observed, would create a new world. We cannot fail to be moved by Tolstoi's uncompromising dedication to his new ideal in every slightest element of his own life: "Whatever else we have or have not in Count Tolstoi, we have at least a great soul and a great writer." But Arnold has one single objection: "Christianity cannot be packed into any set of commandments: . . . Christianity is a *source;* no one supply of water and refreshment that comes from it can be called the sum of Christianity." Tolstoi falls into dogma, in fact. "Jesus paid tribute to the government and dined with the publicans. . . . Perhaps Levine's *provisional solution* [my emphasis], in a society like ours, was nearer to 'the rule of God, of the truth,' than the more trenchant solution which Count Tolstoi has adopted for himself since." Dogma, for Arnold, always runs the risk of its self-righteousness and absoluteness. The world as we know it does not allow the absolute. And Jesus, for Arnold, teaches this lesson against absolutes. In the continual flux of human development, we must make do with the *provisional*, the "convenient supposal" of Glanvill, the fiction of metaphor and myth, as we try to "be good."

Arnold's recognition of Levine's *provisional* proclaims the connection of this Tolstoi essay with *Literature and Dogma*. The novelist can have, like Jesus, a secret and a method, but let him not go in for dogma. Conduct is by far the greater part of religion, and the best conduct is the imitation of Jesus. The novelist, then, can participate in the imitation by extending charity to humblest or the greatest sinner. Arnold sees Tolstoi's novels as a better "imitation" than anything that can be done in doctrinal writings. Above all, by extending his love to his characters he makes us know and love them. Insofar as Arnold is impressed in his English way with Anna's sin, and even so loves her, just so far does he recognize the art of this novelist. He does not mention the Gospel episode of the women taken in adultery, but he might have. Tolstoi presents us with Anna, and turns to us saying, "He that is without sin among you, let him first cast a stone." *There*, now, is a phenomenological theory of the novel waiting to get out of this essay of Arnold's—the reader is implicated, possibly "surprised by sin."

Tolstoi, we are told, "considered Arnold's article . . . to contain well-formulated and justified criticism." Nevertheless, he notoriously exercises a kind of Christian *interestedness*, and frequently it is as though he cannot help being the great writer in spite of it. Oddly, I think one may see the effect of *Literature and Dogma* in his novel *Resurrection* (1899). He began it in the period when he was rereading *Literature and Dogma* (1890–91), and it can be viewed as a kind of Arnoldian paradigm. Nekludoff is compact of two Arnoldian "selves"; *resurrection* is understood in Arnold's way as the metaphor for a new life on earth, and joy is the result of righteousness. But despite all its merit and interest, we must grant as Arnold would (he did not live to read it) that because of the conspicuous doctrine it fails of greatness. *War and Peace* and *Anna Karénine* stay with the provisional and are great *fictions* in more than one sense.

Finally, I think the question of Arnold and God is no other than the question of Arnold and fictions. For him, the time was out of joint, and to set it right was to readjust the religious side of life to the actual and scientific side. The Germans had posited *development* as the way of things, and it became apparent that to accept *development* is to forgo absolute "truth" and to make do with the *provisional*—convenient supposals, fictions. Theological dogma, in claiming to be "true," puts itself forward as science, misapprehending science itself. For the propositions of science, as Glanvill knew and as was becoming more apparent in Arnold's time, are by their nature provisional: new discoveries are perpetually invalidating them, and we must be willing to abandon them and come up with new propositions more "adequate" to the state of knowledge at the time. Since Arnold's time, limitation results and uncertainty principles—relativity, in fact—have obliged scientists more and more to underwrite the principle of provisionality. A hypothesis must not be creed but a policy, which we adopt temporarily as the best basis for the next stage of investigations. The "best" hypothesis, or fiction, is the one that best fits the present sense of the way things are and best meets our needs for action. Arnold's words for value in literature, *pragmatic* and *adequate*, perfectly catch this relativity of value in our fictions.

For Arnold, the greatest challenge of his career was the rationalization of religion; accordingly it is in his religious books that he best realizes his central principle of provisionality, and so they best reveal the principle of all his work. All dogma is vulnerable because [it is] presented as absolute. But what is blessedly *in*vulnerable is literature (or poetry, or art), because it acknowledges its fictionality. It cannot date; rather, it makes past and distant civilizations accessible to us and so extends human community: in Carlyle's words, "It is thus that the Wise Man stands ever encompassed, and spiritually embraced, by a cloud of witnesses and brothers." *Bildung* is the mode that best suits this relative, becoming, provisional world, for *Bildung* acknowledges the flux, recognizes human capacity as distinctively infinite, and wills perpetual cultivation of all distinctively human capacities. Arnold's idea of Culture, then, embracing *Bildung*, subsumes all humane activities: science, politics, art, literature, and religion, all understood in a basically Herderian expressionist way as a series of human constructs. All Arnold's works turn on the great pole not of Bacon's "truth" but of the provisional. *Poetry*, and the word is used more and more in the course of his career to equal *the metaphorical mode*, is the mode of the provisional or of fictions; it is the human way of survival. "I am a stranger here on earth: O hide not thy commandments from me." Poetry *will* prevail. "Currency and supremacy are insured to it, not indeed by the world's deliberate and conscious choice, but by something far deeper—by the instinct of self-preservation in humanity."

A. DWIGHT CULLER

Matthew Arnold and the Zeitgeist

In 1871 Matthew Arnold wrote to Newman at the Oratory expressing the strong "interest with which I used to hear you at Oxford, and the pleasure with which I continue to read your writings now." Then, with a quaint apology for not having become a Catholic, he added, "We are all of us carried in ways not of our own making or choosing, but nothing can ever do away the effect you have produced upon me, for it consists in a general disposition of mind rather than in a particular set of ideas." A few months later he added, "There are four people, in especial, from whom I am conscious of having learnt—a very different thing from merely receiving a strong impression—learnt habits, methods, ruling ideas, which are constantly with me; and the four are— Goethe, Wordsworth, Sainte-Beuve, and yourself. You will smile and say I have made an odd mixture and that the result must be a jumble." Arnold would not, of course, have said directly to Newman what he said in his lecture on Emerson a few years later, that "Cardinal Newman . . . in the Oratory . . . has adopted, for the doubts and difficulties which beset men's minds to-day, a solution which, to speak frankly, is impossible." But though Arnold believed that Roman Catholicism was an anachronism in the modern world, he also deeply admired the ethos and temper of that religion and of the Tractarian movement which led up to it. He saw that Newman and the Tractarians had been doing in the realm of religion what he was trying to do in the realm of culture. The Private Judgment which they regarded as the central error of Protestantism was but a version of the

From *The Victorian Mirror of History.* © 1985 by Yale University. Yale University Press, 1985.

provinciality, the eccentricity, which he regarded as the besetting sin of the English. Both he and they believed that this sin and this error could be rectified only by creating a center of authority whereby the individual could correct and discipline his own nature. But whereas Newman believed that authority was divine, Arnold believed it was human. In a certain sense Arnold believed in the Dogmatic Principle—there was such a thing as Truth, but it was set on a mountain top where human beings could never reach it, though it was appropriate they should spend their lifetime trying. Hence, Arnold could not go along with Newman on the idea of the Visible Church. He saw the logical necessity for it if subjectivity and individualism were to be avoided, and in his essay "The Literary Influence of Academies" he so enlarged upon the value to France of the French Academy that one expected him to recommend a comparable institution for the English. But at the end of the essay he shied away from it and, like Adam, who is to find a "Paradise within thee, happier far," recommended that each individual construct his own personal "academy" through a process of self-discipline and culture.

Arnold was a generation younger than Newman and Carlyle, and hence his youth fell upon the crisis of 1848 rather than that of 1830–33. But in those years he underwent a conversion very similar to Carlyle's and not totally unlike Newman's. His was from the subjectivity and Sturm und Drang of his early poetry to the calm and objectivity of his critical prose, and as with those other writers it provided a paradigm for his conception of history. This conception was initially embodied in a myth which constitutes the central organizing symbol of all his poetry and which continues to undergird his thought even when he moves from poetry into prose. The myth is played out upon a symbolic landscape which is divided into three regions, representing the period of childhood and early youth, the period of young manhood and maturity, and the period of old age or death. In accordance with Arnold's usage, we may call them the Forest Glade, the Burning or Darkling Plain, and the Wide-Glimmering Sea. Through these regions runs the River of Life or Time, carrying both the individual and the whole of humanity from a period of unity of being, when one lived in harmony with nature and oneself, to a period of fragmentation, when one is alienated from God, divorced from nature, and at odds even with one's own soul, to a final period of restored unity, which is a synthesis of the innocence of the first period with the bitter knowledge of the second. Arnold's poetry necessarily regards this myth from the point of view of the second period (the present), looking back nostalgically to the freshness of the early world and forward hopefully to the future. The third period, when it comes, will recover the

Joy of the first period but without its elements of romantic illusion and aristocratic exclusiveness; it will be a "Joy whose grounds are true" and a "Joy in widest commonalty spread." It is a period which Arnold does not reach in his poetry and which is barely adumbrated in his prose.

It is clear that Arnold's myth of history is simply the universal tripartite myth of all who take a tragic view of life. It is related to the cycle of birth, death, and rebirth which was the basis of Greek tragedy, and to the cycle of Paradise, the expulsion from Paradise, and the "Paradise within" which is the substance of Christian myth. Since the third period of the myth is a synthesis of the first two, it may also be considered as forming the first period of a new cycle, and the threefold pattern as accommodating itself to the alternating organic-critical-organic periods of Carlyle and the Saint-Simonians. When Arnold first read Carlyle, he must have felt that his own sense of history was being reinforced, and that the pattern of Teufelsdröckh's idyllic childhood, his Everlasting No with its transitional Center of Indifference, and his Everlasting Yea corresponded to his own three periods. Like Carlyle, Arnold acted out his myth in his own life, and in the volume *Empedocles on Etna, and Other Poems* (1852) he has left us a spiritual autobiography not unlike *Sartor Resartus*.

The central spiritual crisis in Arnold's life, corresponding to the episode in the Rue St. Thomas de l'Enfer in *Sartor*, occurred in September 24 to 27, 1849, when Arnold went on a soul-searching expedition up into the Bernese Alps. He was involved with a girl whom we have hitherto known only as "Marguerite" but whom Park Honan has recently identified as Mary Claude. Mary, born in Berlin of French ancestry, was brought by her father to Liverpool while she was still a child. After his death in 1828 her mother bought a summer home at Rothay Bank, Ambleside, less than a mile from the Arnold home at Fox How, and it was in that way that she and Arnold got acquainted. She was a tall, pale, beautiful girl, very intense, somewhat given to melancholy but concealing her melancholy under a light, mocking laughter. She was devoted to modern French and German literature, and among the authors whom she and Arnold must have read was Étienne Pivert de Senancour, author of the Wertheresque novel *Obermann*. Senancour was one of those second- or even third-generation Romantic writers for whom protest has faded into fretfulness, the "unstrung will" of modern life. Arnold had first encountered his work in 1847 and, feeling that it expressed exactly the mood of his generation, had taken Senancour as the "master of my wandering youth." So much so, indeed, that when he went to Oxford in November 1848 and found himself repelled by the superficiality of the place, he wrote to Clough, "I . . . took up Obermann, and refuged myself with him in his forest against your Zeit Geist." "Better that," he added, "than be sucked for an hour even into the Time Stream in which they and [you] plunge and bellow."

Ultimately, however, it was not the modern Obermann but his ancient counterpart, Empedocles, with whom Arnold refuged himself, for in the summer of 1849 J. C. Shairp wrote to Clough: "I saw the said Hero—Matt—the day I left London. He goes in Autumn to the Tyrol with Slade. He was working at an 'Empedocles'—which seemed to be not much about the man who leapt in the crater—but his name & outward circumstances are used for the drapery of his own thoughts." How much they were so used Shairp would have realized if he could have followed Arnold to Switzerland (his actual destination rather than the Tyrol) and seen him act out his own drama in the Bernese Alps.

This drama involved making some decision about "Marguerite," who had come to represent for Arnold the disturbing element of sexual passion and also a soul which knew not itself in any depth. He also had to decide what kind of person he was and what he was to do. "I am here," he wrote to Clough from Thun, "in a curious and not altogether comfortable state: however tomorrow I carry my aching head to the mountains and to my cousin the Blümlis Alp." The flight to the mountains was evidently for the purpose of self-mastery and self-discovery, for earlier in the letter Arnold had confided to Clough: "What I must tell you is that I have never yet succeeded in any one great occasion in consciously mastering myself: I can go through the imaginary process of mastering myself and see the whole affair as it would then stand, but at the critical point I am too apt to hoist up the mainsail to the wind and let her drive. However as I get more awake to this it will I hope mend . . . [My] one natural craving is not for profound thoughts, mighty spiritual workings etc. etc. but a distinct seeing of my way as far as my own nature is concerned."

The process of self-mastery for Arnold involved putting behind him not only Marguerite but also all other morbid things that troubled without advancing him, and that included Obermann. And so as Arnold walked up into the Obermann country (for Senancour's novel is set partly in the mountains around the Baths of Leuk), he exorcised the spirit of that unproductive thinker. Specifically, he composed the "Stanzas in Memory of the Author of 'Obermann,' " which records, he tells us, "my separation of myself, finally, from him and his influence." This act—the act by which Arnold separated himself from Obermann—was certainly the most important spiritual act of his entire life, for it put behind him all the turbulence and unrest, the Sturm und Drang, that had troubled him in previous years.

Unfortunately, when Arnold exorcised the spirit of Obermann in September 1849, he was already engaged upon his drama *Empedocles on Etna*, which was the very essence of all that he had put behind him. He had chosen Empedocles because, as he said in his Preface, into the feelings of this last of the Greek religious philosophers "there entered much that we are accustomed to consider as exclusively modern; . . . the dialogue of the mind with itself has commenced; modern problems have presented themselves; we hear already the doubts, we witness the discouragement, of Hamlet and of Faust." He was determined to analyze, as lucidly and pitilessly as did Obermann, the modern situation. "Woe was upon me," he wrote to Clough, "if I analysed not my situation: and Werther, Réné, and such like, none of them analyse the modern situation in its true *blankness* and *barrenness*, and *unpoetrylessness*." Shairp had declared that Arnold was merely using the philosopher as a cloak for his own thoughts and feelings, and this is true. But when Arnold reached the top of the mountain, he did not, like Empedocles, throw himself into a volcano. Rather, in rejecting Obermann, he threw his own personal Empedocles into a volcano and came back down, a whole man, to lead a useful life in the cities of the plain. In one sense *Empedocles on Etna* dramatizes what Arnold did, but in another it dramatizes what he did not do. It dramatizes what he was saved from doing by the fact that he did it vicariously in the realm of art.

Of course, he had to do it again and again, for such affirmations are not accomplished once and for all. And although the writing of *Empedocles on Etna* acted as a catharsis for Arnold, he must have been aware, as Goethe was in the case of *Werther*, that upon others it might have a deleterious effect. Therefore in the autumn of 1853 he decided to exorcise Empedocles as he had previously exorcised Obermann. He was led to this decision partly by the example of Froude. Froude, who was four years older than Arnold, had been through his Empedoclean phase three years earlier when he had published his *Nemesis of Faith*, but now he had gotten married, settled down, and was turning himself into a historian. Arnold visited him at his Welsh home of Plas Gwynant in August 1852 and wrote to Clough: "I should like you to see Froude— quantum mutatus! He goes to church, has family prayers—says the Nemesis ought never to have been published etc. etc.—his friends say that he is altogether changed and re-entered within the giron de l'Eglise—at any rate within the giron de la religion chrétienne: but I do not see the matter in this light and think that he conforms in the same sense in which Spinoza advised his mother to conform—and having purified his moral being, all that was mere fume and vanity and love of notoriety and opposition in his proceedings he has abandoned and regrets. This is my view. He is getting more and more literary, and vise au solide instead of beating the air. May we all follow his example!" Arnold did follow Froude's example, for he went straight from Plas Gwynant to Fox How, where, in the month of September, he wrote the preface to *Poems* (1853) in which he repudiated *Empedocles on Etna* and formulated his new poetical creed.

That creed involved the rejection of romantic subjectivism in favor of a more Classical art in which feelings had a "vent in action" and so are resolved. The whole tenor of Arnold's Preface is toward a greater degree of objectivity: through the selection of an action rather than one's own feelings as a subject, through a concern with the architectonics of a work of art rather than its subordinate parts, and through a subordination of language and expression to plot and theme. Unfortunately, the critics saw the issue as Arnold's choice of an ancient rather than a modern subject. For thirty years this had been a burning controversy with the spasmodic poets and their supporters, the "march-of-mind" men, and Arnold's poem had been reviewed unfavorably by several critics for this reason. Arnold felt he could not allow it to be supposed that he was omitting the drama from his new collection in deference to this opinion, and therefore he declared that his real reason was that, being unresolved, it did not "inspirit and rejoice" the reader, as Schiller said art should. It is odd, given the fact that Arnold says explicitly in the Preface that into the feelings of Empedocles there had entered "much that we are accustomed to consider as exclusively modern," that he did not take his father's line of defense and boldly declare that the chronologically ancient is, in this case, philosophically and culturally modern. In the end, he admits that date is of no importance. What is important is that one should have a great action which "powerfully appeal[s] to the great primary human affections: to those elementary feelings which subsist permanently in the race, and which are independent of time." But it ultimately appears that mere antiquity *is* important to Arnold, partly because the modern age is "wanting in moral grandeur" and so does not provide many great actions, partly because the artist treating a modern subject tends to focus on the trivial details of the social scene rather than the essentials of the inward man, and partly because the mere antiquity, the otherness of the past, has a strengthening and steadying effect upon the artist. It takes him out of himself into another world. In other words, the trouble with *Empedocles on Etna*, in Arnold's view, was that it was *too* modern—morbidly so—and although Arnold had doubtless gone to the legend of the Sicilian philosopher because he though he could deal with his problem more easily under that alien guise than if he had written a drama about Obermann or some fictitious hero of his own, still, it was not alien enough. The Sophists were too patently the utilitarians, Callicles too patently the Keatsian poet, Pausanias too patently the bewildered Anglican clergyman, and Empedocles too patently himself.

His father was right that the ancient was modern, but if there were disease then as now, one did not wish to import it.

Arnold dealt more directly with the question of modernity in his lecture "On the Modern Element in Literature," delivered in November 1857 to inaugurate his appointment as Professor of Poetry at Oxford. He had been present fifteen years before when his father delivered his Inaugural Lecture as Professor of Modern History, and he undoubtedly felt that he was in some sense continuing his father's work. Indeed, several years later when he wrote "Rugby Chapel," the elegy to his father, he added to it the date "November 1857" as if to indicate that it was at this point that he had grown into such sympathy with his father as to make that tribute possible. In some ways the Inaugural Lecture is an even greater tribute because it consists almost entirely of his father's ideas. Its central thesis is that modernity is a quality of mind or spirit that may be found in men of any age and that there are periods of antiquity, such as fifth-century Greece and the Augustan Age in Rome, that are more "modern" than relatively recent periods. Arnold exemplifies this by contrasting Thucydides' critical spirit in handling the Peloponnesian War with the fantastic credulousness of Sir Walter Raleigh in his *History of the World*. Children, however, who follow in their father's footsteps like to differentiate themselves from their father, and Arnold did this, as indeed his professorship required, by concentrating upon literature rather than history. Whereas his father had said that by studying the history of these analogous periods we would come to understand our own and then, by purifying and reinvigorating our religious faith, would find the strength to deal with them, the son turned to the literature of those periods for his stay and remedy. He introduced the term "adequacy" ("a term I am always using," he confided to his brother) and asserted that whereas the literature of fifth-century Greece was supremely adequate in the sense that it reflected fully "the highly developed human nature of that age," the literature of the Augustan Age was not adequate. The Augustan Age was in some ways a fuller and more significant period than the Age of Pericles, but of its greatest writers Lucretius is characterized by depression and ennui, Virgil is tinged with an "ineffable melancholy," and Horace, though enchanting to men of taste and cultivation, is without faith, without enthusiasm, and without energy.

It is a little uncertain exactly what Arnold means by "adequacy," for if Horace and Lucretius accurately depict the spiritual malaise of their time, as Arnold seems to suggest they do, then they are adequate interpreters of their age and it is presumably the age itself that is at fault. If, on the other hand, what he means by "adequacy" is the power not merely to reflect the age but in some way to rise above it, to offer an interpretation and criticism of life that is permanently valid, then Arnold needs some other term than "adequacy"—perhaps "high seriousness." It is apparent that this is what Arnold is moving toward, for he declares that the need of any age that calls itself modern is for "intellectual deliverance," and by this deliverance he means an emotionally satisfying synthesis of the vast and confusing array of facts with which such an age is confronted. Sophocles, who "saw life steadily, and saw it whole," presented such a synthesis, but Empedocles, another fifty-century Greek, did not. Both Empedocles and Lucretius were "modern," but neither was "adequate." They represented the complexity of modern life but not a synthesis of that complexity, and by 1857 that is what Arnold wants.

Arnold developed his conception of "adequacy" in a letter to his brother Tom written just six weeks after the delivery of the Inaugural Lecture.

> A great transformation in the intellectual nature of the English, and, consequently, in their estimate of their own writers, is, I have long felt, inevitable. When this transformation comes the popularity of Wordsworth, Shelley, Coleridge, and others, remarkable men as they were, will not be the better for it. I am very much interested in what you say about Pope. I will read the Essay on Criticism again— certainly poetry was a power in England in his time, which it is not now. . . . You ask why is this. I think it is because Pope's poetry was *adequate*, (to use a term I am always using), to Pope's age—that is, it reflected completely the best general culture and intelligence of that age: therefore the cultivated and intelligent men of that time all found something of themselves in it. But it was a poor time, after all— so the poetry is not and cannot be a first-class one. On the other hand our *time* is a first class one—an infinitely fuller richer age than Pope's, but our poetry is not *adequate* to it; it interests therefore only a small body of sectaries. . . . But it is a hard thing to make poetry adequate to a first-class epoch. The eternal greatness of the literature of the Greece of Pericles is that it is the *adequate* expression of a first-class epoch. Shakespeare again, is the infinitely *more than adequate* expression of a *second class* epoch. It is the immense distinction of Voltaire and Goethe, with all their shortcomings, that they approach *near* to being adequate exponents of first-class epochs. And so on— . . . It is singular—but all this is the very matter debated in my inaugural lecture, & the debating of which will be continued in the two next.

The most striking thing in this letter is the different estimate Arnold now gives of his own age. A decade before these were "damned times," but now it is a "first-class epoch." The reason for this is partly that the times really had changed, as England moved from the "hungry forties" into the economic prosperity and serenity of the mid-fifties, and partly that Arnold's personal situation has changed. It is not that he has moved off the burning plain but that he at least sees the wide-glimmering sea in the distance. The age is still characterized by complexity, but this complexity is less a loss of unity of being than it is a challenge to discover a new unity. Thus, the very morbidity which made Empedocles and Lucretius seem so modern now begins to seem a little old-fashioned. At least, Arnold would like to *make* it old-fashioned by putting it further behind him, and the Inaugural Lecture is a repudiation of Lucretius, as the Preface of 1853 was of Empedocles, and the "Stanzas in Memory of the Author of 'Obermann' " was of Obermann. The truly modern, it now appears, will be that literature which, with a full awareness of the complexity of the modern world upon it, will offer "deliverance" from that world into the next phase of being.

Arnold continued to pursue the theme of the "modern element in literature" through the entire first series of his Oxford lectures, tracing it from antiquity up through the Middle Ages. Unfortunately, his knowledge was not equal to the subject and so he never published these lectures. Among the topics treated were the troubadours, Dante, the scholastic philosophy, and feudalism, and it would be interesting to know how he handled them because neither he nor his father considered the Middle Ages to be a "modern" epoch. Doubtless he found the effort strained and unsatisfactory, for in the next year he turned to an author who had been mentioned in the Inaugural Lecture as supremely adequate but less interesting to us because his age is less interesting—Homer. That Homer could offer "intellectual deliverance" to the modern age seemed likely from a story which Arnold found in Robert Wood's *Essay on the Original Genius and Writings of Homer* (1775). Wood says that at the end of the Seven Years' War he waited upon Lord Granville, then President of the Council, with the preliminary articles of the Treaty of Paris and found him so languid "that I proposed postponing my business for another time; but he insisted that I should stay, saying, it could not prolong his life to neglect his duty; and repeating the following passage out of Sarpedon's speech":

Ah, friend, if once escaped from this battle, we were for ever to be ageless and immortal, neither would I fight myself in the foremost ranks, nor would I send thee into the war that giveth men renown, but now—for assuredly ten thousand fates of death

do every way beset us, and these no mortal may escape nor
avoid—now let us go forward, whether we shall give glory to
other men, or others to us.

"His Lordship repeated the last word several times with a calm and deter-
minate resignation; and, after a serious pause of some minutes, he desired
to hear the Treaty read, to which he listened with great attention, and
recovered spirits enough to declare the approbation of a dying statesman (I
use his own words) 'on the most glorious war, and most honourable peace,
this nation ever saw.' "

Lord Granville, of course, quoted Sarpedon's speech in the original
Greek, and so too does Arnold in retelling the story. But the middle classes
of Arnold's day did not know Greek, and therefore the possibility of Homer's
sustaining them, as he did Lord Granville, depends on the adequacy of
translation. Arnold's lectures *On Translating Homer*, then, are concerned with
exactly the same problem as Newman's *Development of Christian Doctrine*. For
if Homer is the supreme source of value standing at the head of the classical
tradition, as revelation is at the head of the Christian tradition, then there
is the problem of Arnold, as there was for Newman, of transmitting that
value substantially unchanged and yet adapted to the modern mind. *Translatio*
is the technical term for the transmission of culture from one civilization to
another, and translation, both in the literal and the extended sense, is exactly
what is here involved. Arnold discovered, as he surveyed the tradition of
English translations of Homer, that it had hitherto been conducted in accordance with the doctrine of accommodation, each translator adapting his
author to the Spirit of the Age— Chapman translating him into Elizabethan,
Pope into neoclassical, Cowper into eighteenth-century Miltonic, and Ma-
ginn and others into romantic ballads in accordance with the theories of Wolf
and the taste of Sir Walter Scott. Worst of all was the most recent translation,
that which was the principal occasion of Arnold's lectures, by F. W. Newman, brother to the great Oratorian—but no more a brother than Esau was
to Jacob —who had translated Homer into the very image of a nineteenth-
century crochety Englishman. F. W. Newman was a very learned Professor
of Latin at University College, London, but he had married a member of a
small dissenting sect, the Plymouth Brethren, had gone on an ill-advised
missionary expedition to Syria, and then had returned to translate *Hiawatha*
into Latin and *Robinson Crusoe* into Latin and Arabic. Not only in religion
but also in lifestyle he was the very "Dissidence of Dissent and the Protestantism of the Protestant Religion," and he was now translating this greatest
of all world classics into a mirror image of himself. How, Arnold wondered,

can the ordinary provincial Englishman lose his provinciality by reading such a work as this?

Arnold's solution was to do as John Henry Newman had done, set up certain Notes or criteria which would distinguish a true development, or translation, from a false. In his view there were four: Homer was rapid, plain and direct in style, plain and direct in ideas, and noble. (In F. W. Newman's view he was "quaint, garrulous, prosaic, and low.") One may concede that Arnold is translating Homer into his own image as much as F. W. Newman is into his, and that the conflict between them is a part of the contest between the two older universities and the new University of London. One may also concede that Arnold's Apollonian conception of Homer, derived from Winckelmann and Goethe, would soon be replaced by a more Dionysian conception, and that his attempt at a "Visible Church"—"the modern Greek scholar of poetical taste"—was unsatisfactory (Newman preferred more scholarship and less taste). Still, Arnold differed from Newman in at least trying to distance Homer from himself rather than engorge him. In writing his tragedy *Merope* he had learned how different the world created by Greek imagination is from our own, and he thought that difference, that sense of otherness, ought to be preserved.

In the end the conflict came down to the question of how archaic was Homer's diction. Did he sound to Sophocles as antiquated as Chaucer sounds to a Victorian? It is fascinating that the question should have taken this form, for one might think that Homer could be translated into modern English on the grounds that there was some time in the past when his Greek sounded modern. But Thomas Arnold had said that ancient authors ought to be translated into the English of the period analogous to their period of civilization. Thus, he would have translated Herodotus into Elizabethan English but Thucydides into modern. Matthew, imitating his father, thinks of himself as standing in fifth-century Athens and wants Homer to sound to him the way it sounded to Sophocles. He cannot accept the idea that Homer is "medieval." He is rather of the age of the King James version of the Bible, and it is in that diction that Arnold would have him clothed. There is, of course, the additional reason that he sees him as a secular version of Scripture.

But if Homer was supremely adequate, he was not really modern. His age did not have the complexity of a modern age, and therefore he could not offer "intellectual deliverance" from it. For this reason, in his next book, the *Essays in Criticism* (1865), Arnold represents himself as a "seeker still," still wandering in the wilderness of modern Philistia and saluting the promised land from afar. "That promised land," he said, alluding to the great creative epochs of Aeschylus and Shakespeare, "it will not be ours to enter, and we shall die in the wilderness: but to have desired to enter it, to have saluted it from afar, is already, perhaps, the best distinction among contemporaries."

The opening essay, "The Function of Criticism at the Present Time," presents a poignant picture of one who lives in "an epoch of dissolution and transformation." The poet Wordsworth has said that the critical faculty is always lower than the creative, and Arnold is acutely aware of the fact that he has not published a volume of poetry for the past ten years. His excuse is that the production of great works of literature "is not at all epochs and under all conditions possible." Literature works with ideas, the best ideas current at the time. "And I say *current* at the time, not merely accessible at the time; for creative literary genius does not principally show itself in discovering new ideas, that is rather the business of the philosopher. The grand work of literary genius is a work of synthesis and exposition, not of analysis and discovery." It is the business of the critical power "in all branches of knowledge . . . to see the object as in itself it really is" and so to establish "an order of ideas, if not absolutely true, yet true by comparison with that which it displaces. . . . Presently these new ideas reach society, the touch of truth is the touch of life, and there is a stir and growth everywhere; out of this stir and growth come the creative epochs of literature."

One might have thought that such an epoch would come out of the stir of the French Revolution, but, on the one hand, the Revolution rushed too directly into practical projects for the improvement of mankind and, on the other, in England it created in opposition to itself an "epoch of concentration," of which Burke was the great voice. On the continent for the past many years the main effort has been a critical effort, but not so in England. England was so frightened by the Revolution and the external danger of Napoleon that it withdrew into itself and fortified itself in the old order. That work of retrenchment and self-protection was the work of the aristocracy, and well have they done it. They had just the firmness and heroic temper of mind to do it well, and it needed to be done. But now the danger is past, and Arnold senses that a new epoch, an "epoch of expansion," is about to open upon his country. For the work of that epoch a new class more receptive to ideas than the aristocracy will be needed, for the qualities now required are not heroic firmness of mind but openness and flexibility of intelligence. England is wandering between two worlds, one dead, the other no longer "powerless to be born" but requiring a great critical effort to be born, and that is "The Function of Criticism at the Present Time." It is obvious that the words *at the Present Time*—the phrase omitted by T. S. Eliot from the title of his comparable essay—are for Arnold the operative words, for at an earlier time, that of Gibbon and Voltaire, for instance, its function might have been quite different—to destroy the old order rather than create the new—and in a later, more poetic time it might have no function at all. But if that later time is ever to be reached, if we are to achieve "deliverance" from modern Philistia, then we need critics who, "by a disinterested endeavour to learn and propagate the best that is known and thought in the world," can establish a current of fresh and true ideas that will make great poetry possible once more. Just as Newman turned at this point from Antiquity to Catholicity, so Arnold turned from Homer to the literature of continental Europe to examine its adequacy for the modern world.

The individual essays of which *Essays in Criticism* is composed had originally been lectures delivered by Arnold as Professor of Poetry at Oxford, and all had then been published in periodicals. But when Arnold suggested to Macmillan that they be collected into a volume, he added, "I am not at all clear that the papers should be printed in the order in which I have put them down." He had put them down simply in the chronological order of their delivery and publication, but when the volume appeared they had been rearranged in what one can only call the order of Arnold's historical myth. That is to say, they are in the order in which their subjects ought to have lived had they followed the intellectual development of the modern world. Thus, after the two opening theoretical essays Arnold had placed first Maurice de Guérin, a French Keatsian poet who had a happy faculty of interpreting nature but not of the moral interpretation of man. He was obviously an inhabitant of the forest glade and, while very charming, was no guide to the modern world. Even less suitable was his sister Eugénie, who lived in the glade of the Roman Catholic religion but, fretting against herself, had not even achieved happiness in that outmoded religion. Heine, the subject of the third essay, was a true inhabitant of the modern world. From his "mattress-grave" in Paris he had shot against the ramparts of Philistinism arrowy shafts of irony and satire. He had been an effective dissolvent of the old European system, but, says Arnold, he was an acrid dissolvent, deficient not only in love but also in dignity and self-respect. Hence, though a brilliant soldier in the war of the liberation of humanity, he was not "an adequate interpreter of the modern world." He offers us "a half-result, for want of moral balance, and of nobleness of soul and character."

At this point—after three subjects on whom he has passed a primarily negative judgment and before the three on whom he will pass a primarily positive judgment—Arnold inserts the pivotal historical essay of the book, "Pagan and Medieval Religious Sentiment." As the title indicates, it is a contrast between the religious sentiment of the pagan world, as exemplified in Theocritus's fifteenth idyll and that of the medieval world, as exemplified in St. Francis's "Canticle of the Sun." The former is the religion of pleasure, gay, natural, cheerful, and it is a very good religion, says Arnold, so long as things are going well. It served Heine beautifully during the early years of his life, but in old age, when he was sick and sorry, he took refuge in irony and satire. This, however, is a refuge for the few, not the many, and it is now asserted that the test of the satisfactoriness of a religion is its ability to minister to the many. In this, Christianity, the religion of sorrow, is vastly superior, but it too, in its extreme of otherworldliness, overruns the normal limits of humanity. Monte Alverno is as far from us as Pompei, the Reformation as the Renaissance. "The poetry of later paganism lived by the senses and understanding; the poetry of medieval Christianity lived by the heart and imagination. But the main element of the modern spirit's life is neither the senses and understanding, nor the heart and imagination; it is the imaginative reason." With this key statement Arnold has moved beyond his initial historical analysis of alternating critical and creative periods into a perception of what the new creative period must be like.

The last three subjects in the book, though all inhabitants of the burning plain, are at least looking forward to the new age. Joubert is for Arnold the very type of the Buried Life, the obscure author whose fame has been suppressed during his own lifetime because he lived in an uncongenial epoch, but who can be recognized by the "outskirmishers" of the next generation, its quick-witted, light-armed troops, as being one of the sacred family, and so rescued and set aside. It is obvious that Arnold regards himself as one of these quick-witted, light-armed troops who is now in the process of rescuing Joubert—bringing the river of his Buried Life to the surface so that it can contribute to the broadening stream flowing on into the future. Spinoza, the subject of the next essay, also looks to the future because he put religion on a basis suitable to the modern mind. Without the mockery of Voltaire or the passion for demolition of Strauss, he made the purely intellectual love of God the summum bonum of life. Thus his works, aridly metaphysical as they are, will soon be recognized as the central point in modern philosophy.

Finally, Marcus Aurelius, chronologically the most remote of all the subjects, is spiritually the most modern—"a truly modern striver and thinker." He was, says Arnold, "perhaps the most beautiful figure in history." Moreover, he was so not in an age of medieval Catholicism, which made it easy for a St. Louis or a King Alfred to be beautiful, but in an age essentially like our own, an age of imperial paganism. In such an age Epictetus could attain to morality but nothing more. Marcus Aurelius, however, could suffuse morality with something like the emotion of Christianity. Still, though he could suffuse morality with emotion, he could not light it up with emotion, as does the New Testament. In this respect he was imperfect, and Arnold ends the essay by noting that it is through this very imperfection that Marcus Aurelius appeals to men today. "It is because he too yearns as they do for something unattained by him." What if he had been able to enter into Christianity? "Vain question!" says Arnold, "yet the greatest charm of Marcus Aurelius is that he makes us ask it. We see him wise, just, self-governed, tender, thankful, blameless; yet, with all this, agitated, stretching out his arms for something beyond—*tendentemque manus ripae ulterioris amore.*"

This is the last sentence in the essay, and it is also the last sentence in the book. We are struck by its resemblance to the last sentence in "The Function of Criticism at the Present Time," where Arnold says, "There is the promised land, towards which criticism can only beckon. That promised land it will not be ours to enter, and we shall die in the wilderness." It is obvious that Arnold has arrived in his quest at the point at which Marcus Aurelius had arrived in his. Each stood on his respective Mt. Pisgah, the one looking into the promised land of Christianity, the other into that new birth of Christianity to be effected by *Literature and Dogma.*

Arnold seems to have begun thinking seriously about history in the mid-1840s, when he subjected himself to an intensive course of reading in the Romantic German philosophers and historians. He was particularly impressed by the idea of the Zeitgeist. The concept of the Spirit of the Age had been introduced into England from French sources about the time of the Revolution of 1830, but now, in the time of the Revolution of 1848, Arnold reintroduced it from German sources. He probably first encountered it in Carlyle, who uses it in "Characteristics" and *Sartor Resartus*, but he seems always to have associated it with Goethe. His first use of it was in a letter to Clough on July 20, 1848: "Goethe says somewhere that the Zeitgeist when he was young caused everyone to adopt the Wolfian theories about Homer, himself included: and that when he was in middle age the same Zeitgeist caused them to leave these theories for the hypothesis of one poem and one author: inferring that in these matters there is no certainty, but alternating dispositions." Fifteen years later he alluded to the same passage in Goethe's *Schriften zur Literatur* (the section entitled "Homer noch einmal [1827]") and went on to say, "Intellectual ideas, which the majority of men take from the age in which they live, are the dominion of this Time-Spirit; not moral and spiritual life, which is original in each individual." Style is also original with the individual. "In a *man*," Arnold wrote to Clough, "style is the saying in the best way *what you have to say*. The *what you have to say* depends on your age." Style he evidently thought of as subjective; the moral and spiritual life, though also unique to the individual, is surely in some degree objective. It is the area in between the subjective and objective—the vast area of human culture—that depends upon the age. The phrase "alternating dispositions" indicates that Arnold was thinking in terms of critical and creative or organic and mechanical periods.

The phrase "Zeitgeist" differs from the "Spirit of the Age" in its greater emphasis on Time and therefore change. It notes that the Spirit of the Age changes continuously with the passage of time, although it may be only at moments of revolutionary change, as in 1830 and 1848, that people become conscious of the fact and comment upon it. As to why change occurs, Arnold does not say. There is a large fatalistic element in his thought, and the image of the River of Life or Time, which is as pervasive in his prose as in his poetry, suggests that change is simply a cosmic process. It is an aspect of Time. Without change, external or internal, there would be no Time. In the area of knowledge, though not in that of the arts, Arnold believes in progress, though perhaps only *en ligne spirale*, as Goethe did. But in other areas he suggests a law of action and reaction, possibly because life, as he sees it, is a harmonious balance of opposing qualities. Hence, whenever one element, such as Hebraism, becomes dominant there is a natural reaction in favor of its opposite, Hellenism. This law is thus a self-protective device on the part of life itself to preserve the good health of the organism. It is a kind of spiritual sensor which detects in advance changes which need to be made by the body politic if it is to be in harmony with its own inward life. For Arnold agrees with Carlyle that changes are initially spiritual and that the forms of society (Carlyle's "clothes") are continually lagging behind. He does not frequently use his father's analogy between the life of the individual and the history of the world, but he certainly thinks of society as alive and as changing because it is alive.

The changes society undergoes are both positive and negative, for the Time-Spirit is both a Creator and a Destroyer. Fraser Neiman, who has studied this matter in detail, says that Arnold had two widely differing conceptions of the Zeitgeist, in the forties thinking of it as "the temper of the times, with the additional idea that time is a local, changeable phenomenon opposing eternal values;" in the seventies, when he was writing on the Church and the Bible, thinking of it as "an aspect of the eternal, promoting change as a manifestation of its own being." It may be, however, that it was not Arnold's conception of the Zeitgeist that changed but rather the position from which he viewed it. When Arnold felt himself on the burning plain, he necessarily found the Zeitgeist inimical and attempted to refuge himself from it; but when he felt he was approaching the wide-glimmering sea, then the Zeitgeist was working in his favor and he naturally elevated it to a cosmic process. It was the same power in both cases, but in the one operating as the destroyer of the old world, in the other as the creator of the new.

Throughout his life Arnold varied in his view of the Time-Spirit, sometimes regarding it as a mere metaphor for collective shifts in human opinion and sometimes hypostatizing it as a real entity that produced those shifts. He tells his sister, for example, "It is only in the best poetical epochs (such as the Elizabethan) that you can descend into yourself and produce the best of your thought and feeling naturally . . . ; for then all the people around you are more or less doing the same thing. It is natural, it is the bent of the time to do it; its being the bent of the time, indeed, is what makes the time a *poetical* one." The Elizabethan age is poetical *because* many people were then writing and reading poetry. On the other hand, in *St. Paul and Protestantism* Arnold makes the Zeitgeist independent of individual human actions, identifying it with the logic or life in ideas themselves. He associates it with the power which Newman made responsible for the development of Christian doctrine and with St. Paul's "divine power *revealing* additions to what we possess already." The ambiguity of Arnold's feeling is apparent in the fact that he sometimes uses the phrase Zeitgeist along with another phrase—"the 'Zeit-Geist' and the general movement of men's religious ideas" or "the 'Zeit-Geist' and the mere spread of what is called *enlightenment*"—where one cannot tell whether the second phrase is in addition to or in explanation of the first. Generally speaking, in view of Arnold's (along with Goethe's) "imperturbable naturalism" one is inclined to think that the reification of the Time-Spirit is less a matter of real belief on Arnold's part than of rhetorical strategy. Just as he will personify Culture or Criticism in order to give authority to his own ideas and will chastise the provinciality of the English by telling them what "Europe" thinks of them, so here he undertakes to speak for "History." The Time-Spirit is a device whereby Arnold can project his own sense of change onto a persona that is simply irresistible. The change is coming whether people like it or not. On the other hand, when Arnold defines God as "the stream of tendency by which all things seek to fulfill the law of their being," one does not feel that this is a mere rhetorical strategy. There is a distinct element in Arnold that reaches forward to a Bergsonian Life Force, and the only Absolute he really believes in is placed within the evolving forms of life itself. He may mythologize the Time-Spirit for rhetorical purposes, but when he divinizes it, he is probably being serious.

The Time-Spirit embodies itself in external institutions and then, moving on, creates a sense of discordancy between these institutions and its own inner life. This discordancy grows until at last the institutions break up, either rapidly by revolution or more slowly by gradual change, and at such times we feel we are at the end of an era. Thus, the periodization of history is created by the breakup of systems rather than by the more or less constant movement of the Zeitgeist itself.

It is sufficiently obvious that this view of history derives from the Philosophy of Clothes in Carlyle's *Sartor Resartus* and from his German and French sources. Some scholars have perceived in Arnold's work the influence of Vico, but Arnold never quotes Vico, and although the *Scienza Nuova* appears in his reading lists for 1876, there is no evidence he read it. He of course knew his father's "Essay on the Social Progress of States," but his father had so far modified Vico, reducing his Ages of Gods, Heroes, and Men to periods dominated by the aristocracy, the middle class, and the populace, that there was little left peculiar to the Italian. Both father and son did, of course, hold that every society, at least ideally, goes through a threefold evolution and therefore that modern societies tend to repeat the development of those in antiquity. To that extent they are Viconian. But Arnold could have gotten this scheme more easily from Goethe and Carlyle.

Like his predecessors, he does not apply the scheme rigorously or systematically. The alternating epochs tend to fall into a threefold dialectical pattern, but this is not always the case. Moreover, the pattern may be on a very extended time-scale, as with the great divisions of the Middle Ages, the Renaissance, and modern times, or it may be so reduced that epochs of concentration and expansion come and go with bewildering rapidity. In all likelihood Arnold believed that there are cycles within the great cycles of human history, even down to the cycles of individual human life. Thus, though the Middle Ages is a kind of childhood of the world, followed by a harsh maturity from the Elizabethan age on, Romanticism is certainly a miniature childhood within that larger cycle. Moreover, it should be understood that individual nations do not necessarily move in phase. England in 1848 was *"far behind* the Continent," according to Arnold, and the French Revolution, which produced an epoch of expansion in the country in which it occurred, provoked in England an epoch of concentration. Even within a country the various aspects of national life were not always in phase, and it goes without saying that Arnold held different views of different periods at different times. He had a particularly hard time making up his mind about the Elizabethan period, whether it was, as he said in his letter to Tom, a "second-class epoch" with an occasional genius like Shakespeare or one of the great synthetic periods of world history like its counterpart in Italy. Arnold read much history and thought deeply about it, but he was neither an accurate historian of the past nor a systematic philosopher of history. His aim was to draw from the past a paradigm of the stages through which nations and individuals ideally would pass in realizing their full potential.

Arnold applied his philosophy of history in three main areas, the evolution of political society, the course of literary culture, and the history of religion. As might be expected, his terminology and concepts vary from one field to another. In the area of politics Arnold believed, along with his father, that society was moving inevitably towards a greater degree of democracy. Thus, it would evolve through periods dominated by the aristocracy, the middle class, and the populace. But whereas his father believed that in 1830 England was at the crisis point between the second phase and the third, Arnold regarded the process as much less advanced and likely to be less catastrophic. He acknowledged that 1688 was an important date but held that the aristocracy was still well in charge through 1815 and that even after the first Reform Bill the actual reins of government were in their hands. The problem now was to persuade them to relinquish their power, for as Arnold looked back through history he thought he saw that the Roman aristocracy had fallen because it was unable to deal with the idea of the mature period of Roman history after the Punic Wars, and that the Venetian and French aristocracies had fallen because they were unable to deal with the idea of modern Europe. An aristocracy is naturally unsympathetic to ideas, which it regards as visionary and even dangerous, and thus, as the old order ceases to satisfy, there is a need for a new class to come into power that will be sympathetic to ideas. This will be the middle class, and despite Arnold's recognition of the narrowness and lack of intelligence of this group, he believes that it does have the capacity for that role. The "master-thought" of his political writings is the need to educate the middle class so that it can properly perform its role in history. As for the ultimate transfer of power to the people, that is a more distant event which Arnold regards with some unease but as in itself desirable.

In his literary essays Arnold initially used the Goethean-Carlylean terminology of critical and creative periods, saying, in *On Translating Homer* and "The Function of Criticism at the Present Time," that the main effort of the intellect of Europe, for now many years, has been a critical effort, and that the exercise of the creative power in the production of great works of literature is, in the present epoch, simply impossible. But then, a little way into the essay, Arnold shifts to "epochs of concentration" and "epochs of expansion," doubtless because these have a broader cultural application. The two sets of terms are not identical. An epoch of concentration is that great centripetal movement in society whereby a culture draws in upon itself, orders and consolidates its world-view, and defends that view against external enemies long after it has ceased to be alive. It is the epoch of aristocracies, and although it presupposes an earlier act of creation, it really comprehends only the last phase of that act and the first, destructive phase of criticism. An epoch of expansion, on the other hand, is the great centrifugal movement whereby a culture creates, initially through criticism, a new world view which it then enhances and brings into relation with the lives of men through artistic creation. Arnold differs from Carlyle primarily in his insistence that criticism is creative too and, living as he did a generation later than Carlyle, in his emphasis on its creative rather than its destructive aspect. His terms focus on the systole and diastole of human society rather than on the moment of stasis when either criticism or creation is at its height.

It is not difficult to relate these terms to Arnold's political thought. The epoch of concentration is that of the fading of the aristocracy and the epoch of expansion that of the rise of the middle class, but presumably at some time in the future there will be a new epoch of concentration as the middle class attempts to hold on to its power against the new expansive movement of the populace. There is a certain sense in which the three social classes correspond to the three regions of Arnold's imaginative world, for the aristocracy is the childhood of the world, the middle class is transitional, and democracy is the period in which joy will be "in widest commonalty spread." But Arnold's experience of history is limited to the first two classes, and so he tends to see the new expansive movement of the middle class (it is not irrelevant that it is his own class) as the "wide-glimmering sea." He records its coming very precisely in his essays. In the *Essays in Criticism* (1864–65) he is living in "an epoch of dissolution and transformation"—the last phase of an epoch of concentration—and the promised land is far in the distance. "But epochs of concentration cannot well endure for ever; epochs of expansion, in the due course of things, follow them. Such an epoch of expansion seems to be opening in this country." Five years later it apparently had opened, for in *Culture and Anarchy* (1869) Arnold asks, "Is not the close and bounded intellectual horizon within which we have long lived and moved now lifting up, and are not new lights finding free passage to shine in upon us? For a long time there was no passage for them. . . . But now the iron force of adhesion to the old routine . . . has wonderfully yielded." And a few pages later he speaks of "epochs of expansion . . . , such as that in which we now live." In 1880 he reiterated his entire doctrine in a letter to M. Fontanes, the French critic, and in 1886 declared, "The epoch of concentration has ended for us, the ice has broken up." "We are living in an epoch of expansion."

Arnold seems never to have applied the terms *epoch of concentration* and *epoch of expansion* to any except the modern period, but in *Culture and Anarchy* he devised another set of terms which he could use of the entire course of civilization. Hebraism and Hellenism originally denote two constituent elements in human nature: on the one hand, the impulse to right conduct, obedience to God, and strictness of conscience; on the other, the impulse toward intelligence, seeing the object as it really is, and spontaneity of consciousness. But because these two elements are embodied, the one in the Judaeo-Christian, the other in the Graeco-Roman tradition, they may also be observed in human history. They have but one aim, human perfection, but they pursue this aim by different means and each is disposed to regard itself not as a contribution to the whole but as the *unum necessarium*, the one thing needful. Therefore history has proceeded by alternating epochs, in which an exclusive pursuit of one quality has led to a practical neglect of the other and so produced a reaction into the opposite error, which had to be corrected in turn. The bright promise of Hellenic culture, for example, was ultimately found to be unsound simply because it had not provided the indispensable basis of conduct and self-control. It led into the moral enervation and self-disgust of late paganism. In that context Christianity, a more inward and spiritual form of Hebraism, came as a rebirth of the human spirit, but it led, through the austerities of St. Paul, into medieval asceticism and so provoked the Renaissance, a second phase of Hellenism. Arnold pondered deeply about the Renaissance and its relation to the Reformation. He sharply disagreed with Froude that "the Reformation caused the Elizabethan literature." It was rather that "both sprang out of the active animated condition of the human spirit in Europe at that time. After the fall of the Roman Empire the barbarians powerfully turned up the soil of Europe— and after a little time when the violent ploughing was over and things had settled a little, a vigorous crop of new ideas was the result." The Reformation was the "subordinate and secondary side" of the Renaissance, and though it was a Hebraising revival within the church, it was so infused with the subtle Hellenic spirit that "the exact respective parts, in the Reformation, of Hebraism and of Hellenism, are not easy to separate." This great hybrid movement, in other words, which initiated the modern world, was in some degree a synthesis of antiquity and the Middle Ages. Nonetheless, even with the Reformation, the Renaissance had its side of moral weakness, just as later paganism had, and in England Puritanism came as the reaction of Hebraism

against this weakness precisely as primitive Christianity had at the time of
St. Paul.

> Yet there is a very important difference between the defeat in-
> flicted on Hellenism by Christianity eighteen hundred years ago,
> and the check given to the Renascence by Puritanism. . . . Eigh-
> teen hundred years ago it was altogether the hour of Hebraism.
> Primitive Christianity was legitimately and truly the ascendant
> force in the world at that time, and the way of mankind's progress
> lay through its full development. Another hour in man's devel-
> opment began in the fifteenth century, and the main road of his
> progress then lay for a time through Hellenism. Puritanism was
> no longer the central current of the world's progress, it was a
> side stream crossing the central current and checking it.

If one asks how Arnold knows that it is a side stream, his reply is that it is
only in England that this happened. On the continent Hellenism remained
the dominant movement from the Renaissance to the present time, but in
England, in the seventeenth century, the middle class "entered the prison
of Puritanism, and had the key turned upon its spirit there for two hundred
years." If Arnold were speaking to the French, he would doubtless recommend some additional Hebraism, but speaking to the English, he recom-
mends their peculiar deficiency, Hellenism.

Though both Hebraism and Hellenism have both critical and creative
phases, Hebraism, as Arnold views it, is often simply the moral and religious
aspect of an epoch of concentration and Hellenism the cultural aspect of an
epoch of expansion. The new terms have the virtue, however, of denoting
the powers which produce this systole and diastole of human history and so
are more useful for tracing the development of civilization. But Arnold also
needs to analyze a development within the Hebraic tradition, and for this
he turns, in *Literature and Dogma*, to another set of terms, verifiable religious
experience *vs. Aberglaube*.

The Bible, in Arnold's view, is not a theological work which sets forth
in precise, scientific terms the dogmas of the Christian religion, but is simply
the literature of the Hebrew people. Like any literature it is couched in the
language of metaphor and symbol, for these alone could shadow forth the
profound spiritual experiences of the Old Testament prophets. At least in
the early golden years the people had no difficulty interpreting it. Gradually,
however, as they suffered misfortunes and weakened in faith, they began to
interpret these insights literally, to look for a miraculous change that would
restore their fallen fortunes—to expect a Messiah. These new beliefs were

not such as could be verified by experience. They were "extra-beliefs"—
Aberglaube—not exactly superstitions but beliefs *in addition* to what they knew
by their own experience of the moral law to be true. When the Messiah did
come, then, his function was not to fulfill this mechanical religion but to
renew and deepen the experience on which true religion was based—to renew
it by the method of inwardness, the secret of renunciation, and the mildness
of his own temper. Unfortunately, his followers were once again prone to
take literally what he meant only spiritually, and so once again a new *Aberglaube*, that of Christian theology, grew up. By Arnold's day it had become
so entangled in metaphysics and the supernatural that the masses of men
were ready to reject the Bible altogether rather than believe what they were
told it meant. And so Arnold, who believed the Bible was the greatest
repository of spiritual wisdom the world possessed, broke through this web
of musty theology to re-present the Bible, as Coleridge and his father had
before him, as the religious experience of the Hebrew people. So viewed,
the joy announced by Christ would become a "joy whose grounds are true"
and so would once again be accepted by the masses, as a "joy in widest
commonalty spread." Far more truly than by the advent of democracy or of
a new Hellenism, this would bring about the New Heavens and the New
Earth that Arnold desired.

The period that Arnold found most analogous to this own was the period
of late paganism immediately before the birth of Christ. For twenty years
Arnold tried to write a tragedy on Lucretius, for he found the passage at
the end of the third book where Lucretius depicts the tedium and ennui of
the Roman noble, driving furiously abroad in order to escape from himself
and then driving furiously home again, one of the most powerful and solemn
in all literature. He quoted it in his lecture "On the Modern Element in
Literature" and used it again in "Obermann Once More." To Clough he
wrote in 1835, "We deteriorate in spite of our struggle—like a gifted Roman
falling on the uninvigorating atmosphere of the decline of the Empire." The
later period covered by Gibbon he was not so interested in, but when he
was passing through Arles in the south of France, he wrote to his sister, "I
cannot express to you the effect which this Roman south of France has upon
me—the astonishing greatness of the ancient world, of which the provincial
corners were so noble—its immense superiority to the Teutonic middle age—
its gradual return, as civilization advances, to the command of the world—
all this, which its literature made me believe in beforehand, impresses itself
upon my senses when I see these Gallo Roman towns. I like to trace a certain
affinity in the spirit of these buildings between the Romans and the English;
'you and the Romans,' Guizot said to me the other day, 'are the only two

governing nations of the world.' " This was in 1859; a dozen years earlier he had written in his notebook:

> The Roman world perished for having disobeyed reason and nature.
>
> The infancy of the world was renewed with all its sweet illusions.
>
> but infancy and its illusions must for ever be transitory, and we are again in the place of the Roman world, our illusions past, debtors to the service of reason & nature.
>
> O let us beware how we again are false to them: we shall perish, and the world will be renewed: but we shall leave the same questions to be solved by a future age.

In "Obermann Once More," alluding to the birth-time of Christianity, he said,

> 'Oh, had I lived in that great day,
> How had its glory new
> Fill'd earth and heaven, and caught away
> My ravish'd spirit too!'

But he added that in the modern rebirth of Christianity one must remain "unduped of fancy," lest one be doomed to repeat the Middle Ages all over again.

Of the Middle Ages Arnold wrote to his sister, "I have a strong sense of the irrationality of that period, and of the utter folly of those who take it seriously, and play at restoring it; still, it has poetically the greatest charm and refreshment possible for me. The fault I find with Tennyson in his *Idylls of the King* is that the peculiar charm and aroma of the Middle Age he does not give in them. There is something magical about it, and I will do something with it before I have done." Oxford, "steeped in sentiment as she lies, spreading her gardens to the moonlight, and whispering from her towers the last enchantments of the Middle Age," was for Arnold the very symbol of that magic, but it was also the "home of lost causes, and forsaken beliefs, and unpopular names, and impossible loyalties"—in particular, of Newman, who had vainly attempted to revive there the dream of the Catholic Church. Of the Celtic people, whom Arnold treated in his lectures *On the Study of Celtic Literature*, the bard had said, "They went forth to the war, *but they always fell*." They were characterized by sentiment, the willful rebellion against the despotism of fact, and though they contributed to English poetry its element of "natural magic," they contributed nothing more. The Middle

Ages was the childhood of the modern world, and though one might yearn for the beauty and charm of one's childhood, it was impossible to return. It was impossible to return to the monastery of the Grande Chartreuse, whose religion offered a refuge, but the refuge of the tomb. One of Arnold's sharpest criticisms of the romantic poets was that they did seek to return. When he wished to say that Wordsworth "voluntarily cut himself off from the modern spirit," he said that he "retired (in Middle-Age phrase) into a monastery." At the same time "Scott became the historiographer-royal of feudalism," and Coleridge took to opium. The same was true of the German romantics. Carlyle had declared that Tieck, Novalis, Richter, and others were the chief inheritors and continuators of Goethe's work, but Arnold declared that they were a minor current; the main current flowed from Goethe to Heine. "The mystic and romantic school of Germany lost itself in the Middle Ages, was overpowered by their influence, came to ruin by its vain dreams of renewing them. Heine, with a far profounder sense of the mystic and romantic charm of the Middle Age than Görres, or Brentano, or Arnim, Heine the chief romantic poet of Germany, is yet also much more than a romantic poet: he is a great modern poet, he is not conquered by the Middle Age, he has a talisman by which he can feel,—along with but above the power of the fascinating Middle Age itself,—the power of modern ideas."

To Arnold the Renaissance put European civilization back upon the right road after the long detour of the Middle Ages. He quotes again and again in his notebooks the remark of Renan, "*La Renaissance—ce grand éveil, qui replaçait l'humanité dans la voie des grandes choses*"; and again, "*The Renaissance le retour à la vrai tradition de l'humanité civilisée.*" Uniting as it did Hebraism and Hellenism, the senses and understanding of late antiquity with the heart and imagination of the Middle Ages, it was one of the great epochs of the "imaginative reason," the beginning of the modern world. Moreover, Arnold had somehow persuaded himself that the high culture of the Renaissance pervaded a large body of the community, creating a current of fresh ideas, and that it is this broad basis of culture that is "the secret of rich and beautiful epochs in national life; the epoch of Pericles in Greece, the epoch of Michael Angelo in Italy, the epoch of Shakespeare in England." It created a "national glow of life and thought" that made for a great creative and expansive epoch. Raphael, Arnold thought, was probably the ideal representative of this age, but unfortunately Arnold knew little about Raphael or Michelangelo, and so he had to confine himself to his own country. There he was less enthusiastic. Though he never said publicly what he said in a private letter to Tom, that the Elizabethan Age was a "second-class epoch" (indeed, he always acknowledged that it was England's greatest), he did not consider it really modern. It retained too much of the Middle Ages upon it, had not really entered into the classical decorum. Or rather, having been so long repressed by the Middle Ages, it burgeoned forth into a fantasticality and playfulness that was simply extravagant. It did so partly because it did not have a complex body of thought and feeling to wrestle with and so could devote itself to curious and exquisite expression. For this reason Arnold did not think it provided a good model for the modern poet. "More and more I feel that the difference between a mature and a youthful age of the world compels the poetry of the former to use great plainness of speech as compared with that of the latter: and that Keats and Shelley were on a false track when they set themselves to reproduce the exuberance of expression, the charm, the richness of images, and the felicity of the Elizabethan poets." Indeed, the literature of the eighteenth century was simply "a long reaction against this eccentricity," and ultimately it perished through its own provinciality. On the continent, however, Goethe and Voltaire had created a great critical effort which, in the completeness of its culture, was almost the equivalent of a true creative age. It only lacked the "national glow of life and thought" which one finds when ideas are widely diffused among the people and not derived from books. Moreover, it was in the eighteenth century that Hellenism, checked by the Puritan reaction, achieved its full development, and Arnold was strangely drawn to the period. "I am glad you like Gray," he wrote to his wife; "that century is very interesting, though I should not like to have lived in it; but the people were just like ourselves, whilst the Elizabethans are not."

The truly great synthetic epoch in the past is the Periclean Age in Athens. "There is a century in Greek life," wrote Arnold, "the century preceding the Peloponnesian war, from about the year 530 to the year 430 B.C.,—in which poetry made, it seems to me, the noblest, the most successful effort she has ever made as the priestess of the imaginative reason, of the element by which the modern spirit, if it would live right, has chiefly to live. Of this effort . . . the four great names are Simonides, Pindar, Aeschylus, Sophocles." Arnold does not claim that these poets are perfect, but no other poets have so well balanced the thinking power by the religious sense. As he contemplates their work, he is impressed by their objective excellence and solidity: they are like a group of statuary seen at the end of a long dark vista. "I know not how it is," he says in the Preface to *Poems* (1853), "but their commerce with the ancients appears to me to produce, in those who constantly practise it, a steadying and composing effect upon their judgment, not of literary works only, but of men and events in general. They are like persons who have had a very weighty and impressive experience: they are more truly than others under the empire of facts, and more independent of the language current among those with whom they live." The Periclean Age is modern in the sense that it has a deep, inward affinity with contemporary life, but it rises so far above the level of that life that it is an ideal rather than an analogy.

In his later years Arnold turned more and more from the Greeks to the Hebrew scriptures. Indeed, he had no sooner recommended an increase of Hellenism to the English people than he began to think that an increase of Hebraism was what they needed. "If I was to think only of the Dissenters," he wrote to Kingsley in 1870, "or if I were in your position, I should press incessantly for more Hellenism; but, as it is, seeing the tendency of our *young* poetical litterateur (Swinburne), and on the other hand, seeing much of Huxley . . . , I lean towards Hebraism, and try to prevent the balance from on this side flying up out of sight." It was, of course, balance that Arnold was trying to maintain. He was in no sense a relativist, saying that whatever the Zeitgeist brought was to be accounted a blessing. It was rather that the whole course of history presented an ideal of totality or comprehensiveness, the harmonious development of one's powers that was lacking in any particular age. It was also lacking in any particular nation. Just as Newman sought the note of Catholicity by looking to Rome and the note of Apostolicity by looking to Jerusalem, so Arnold also sought these values by looking, on the one hand, to the modern civilizations of France and Germany and, on the other, to the Graeco-Roman tradition. But after the Franco-Prussian War of 1870 he became increasingly disgusted with the modern French. *Madame Bovary* was not to be recommended, and Balzac, unlike Arnold's beloved George Sand, was to be deplored. Whereas previously the French had been characterized by their widespread intelligence, they were now a nation of *hommes sensuels moyens* who worshipped the goddess Lubricity, and their downfall was only a matter of time. "[It] is mainly due" wrote Arnold to his mother, "to that want of a serious conception of righteousness and the need of it, the consequences of which so often show themselves in the world's history, and in regard to the Graeco-Latin nations more particularly. The fall of Greece, the fall of Rome, the fall of the brilliant Italy of the fifteenth century, and now the fall of France, are all examples." Earlier it was the inability to cope with modern ideas that had produced these downfalls.

As Arnold swung back from the Latin to the Saxon races and from Hellene to Hebrew, he turned increasingly to the Old Testament. In 1872 he published an edition of the Second Isaiah for school use and declared in the Introduction that the work provided a key to "universal history." "Many of us have a kind of centre-point in the far past to which we make things converge, from which our thoughts of history instinctively start and to which they return; it may be the Persian War, or the Peloponnesian War, or Alexander, or the Licinian Laws, or Caesar. Our education is such that we are strongly led to take this centre-point in the history of Greece or Rome; but it may be doubted whether one who took the conquest of Babylon [538 B.C.] and the restoration of the Jewish exiles would not have a better. Whoever began with laying hold on this series of chapters [40–66] as a whole, would have a starting-point and lights of unsurpassed value for getting a conception of the course of man's history and development as a whole." Here, then, is an alternative to the Age of Pericles, the slightly earlier age of the Second Isaiah. One reason that Arnold so prized it was that the majority of people require joy in their literature, "and if ever that 'good time coming,' for which we all of us long, was presented with energy and magnificence, it is in these chapters" of the Second Isaiah. Hence, in the lecture "Numbers," which Arnold delivered on his tour of America, he contrasted Plato's conception of the "remnant," the small band of honest followers who, in the madness of the multitude, seek shelter under a wall till the storm is over and then depart in mild and gracious mood, with Isaiah's "remnant" (in this case the first Isaiah's), who will actually restore the state. Isaiah's hope is foolish, says Arnold, for the numbers, either in Athens or in Israel, are far too small. But Arnold's father had told him that numbers were the characteristic of democracy, and so in America's fifty millions there will perhaps be found a remnant of sufficient magnitude to accomplish the task.

Arnold's conception of the remnant seems overstrained and dubious, but it is not unrelated to a conception much more fundamental to his thought, that of the lonely individual who carries on, in a climate uncongenial to his genius, to transmit to the future the values of civilization. Such a man was Marcus Aurelius, a "truly modern striver and thinker" who nonetheless had "a sense of constraint and melancholy" upon him because he longed for something more than his age could provide. Such a man was Falkland, a martyr of moderation and tolerance amid the violence of the English civil war. "Shall we blame him for his lucidity of mind and largeness of temper?" By no means. "They are what make him ours; what link him with the nineteenth century. He and his friends, by their heroic and hopeless stand against the inadequate ideals dominant in their time, kept open their communications with the future, lived with the future." Such a person was Gray, a born poet who fell upon an age of prose and so "never spoke out." "Coming when he did, and endowed as he was, he was a man . . . whose spiritual flowering was impossible. The same thing is to be said of his great contemporary, Butler." It maybe said too of Joubert, who, though passing with scant notice through his own generation, was singled out by the light-armed troops of the next as a person to be preserved and, like the lamp of life itself, handed on to the next generation. It is as one of these that Arnold saw himself, not as a great poet but as one who, living in the days of the Philistines, yet kept his gift pure and so was a forerunner, a preparer, an initiator of the age to come.

"I think," Arnold wrote to his sister in 1863, "in this concluding half of the century the English spirit is destined to undergo a great transformation; or rather, perhaps I should say, to perform a great evolution." He never ceased to think so or to aid in that evolution. Unlike some of his contemporaries he did not settle down into a fixed position as old age came upon him. By looking to the past he kept himself oriented toward the future. He had in his mind's eye the image of a society in which the whole body of men should come to live with a life worthy to be called *human*. "This, the humanisation of man in society, is civilisation." He knew, however, that this ideal was simply to be sought; it would never be reached once and for all. "Undoubtedly we are drawing on towards great changes; and for every nation the thing most needful is to discern clearly its own condition, in order to know in what particular way it may best meet them. Openness and flexibility of mind are at such a time the first of virtues. *Be ye perfect*, said the Founder of Christianity. . . . Perfection will never be reached; but to recognise a period of transformation when it comes, and to adapt themselves honestly and rationally to its laws, is perhaps the nearest approach to perfection of which men and nations are capable."

SARA SULERI

Entropy on Etna:
Arnold and the Poetry of Reading

"Amongst a *people* of readers the literature is a greater engine than the philosophy," Arnold wrote to Arthur Hugh Clough in 1848, a year before the publication of his first volume of poems, *The Strayed Reveller*. Such aggressive assertion indicates how early Arnold wanted to believe in the efficacy of a literature that, while distinct from philosophic discourse, could be subsumed into a rhetoric of philosophy and further emphasizes how such a merger would be dependent on a receptive body of readers. This anxious claim extends through the rhetorical dilemmas of Arnold's own poetry to his later critical writing, in which literature is presented as a substitute for religion and philosophy, and a new attitude towards reading is stressed as the only means to make that substitution possible. In attempting to alleviate the "unpoetical" iron age he inhabited, Arnold consciously assumes the role of a Wordsworthian "attentive reader," whose function is not to produce philosophic systems but to effectively "extract" them from the texts of others. Throughout Arnold's writing, both in his poetry and prose works, the figure of reader is linked to poetic possibility in a swerve that encompasses two of Arnold's most characteristic positions: on one level, a reader is in a superior place of authority and control in that he can judge and organize literary texts into a coherent philosophic whole and can act as an editor to assemble touchstones of the best that is known and thought in the world. On another level, the Arnoldian reader is always "only" a reader, whose perpetually secondary position illustrates that he has neither a new discourse nor the old faith of his predecessors, and that he will consequently die in the wilderness.

The sense of defeated authority implicit in this dialectic is often attributed to Arnold's desire to be a prototype of the modern alienated mind, but an acquiescence with the narcissism of Arnold's narrative overlooks his tendency to compensate for a sense of philosophic lack by producing a system of reading that serves as the practical equivalent of a philosophic mirage. I seek to study the strategies of substitution and compensation that constitute Arnold's poetic method and to trace the patterns through which a rhetoric of philosophic mobility is made available by his fierce embrace of the idea of readership.

While the importance that Arnold attaches to reading has been extensively studied in reference to his criticism and his discourse on culture, it is less frequently identified in the slight lyricism of his poetry, in which context it is usually interpreted as a sign of his irretrievably "academic" nature. Thus to Eliot, Arnold's emphasis on books and reading is proof of the fact that "he had neither walked in hell nor been rapt to heaven; but what he did know, of books and men, was in its way well-balanced and well-marshalled." In Henry James's more perceptive view, this emphasis is not necessarily a limitation: he notes in Arnold's poetry a "constant reference to nature, or to Wordsworth, which is almost the same thing, but there is an even more implicit reference to civilization, literature, and the intellectual experience of man." Rather than illustrating his "bookish" flavor, this implicit reference in Arnold's poetry indicates one of the major strategies that he adopted to deal with an age that was "not unprofound, not ungrand, not unmoving:— but *unpoetical*." In a historical narrative that Arnold saw lacking in both "certitude and joy" and a "certain order of ideas" to feed and sustain writing, the idiom of orderliness is only duplicated by a poet who assumes the position of a reader who can at least interpret, recall, and contemplate lost systems of belief. Arnold's major poems are thus explicit or implicit readings of his precursors and the systems they represent in which the very act of admiration serves as philosophic consolation. The early sonnet, "To a Friend," provides a clear model of this tactic. The opening question illustrates the disarray in syntax and in the available vocabulary of Arnold's intellectual environment: "Who props, thou ask'st, in these bad days, my mind?" The response comes rapidly and authoritatively: Homer, Epictetus, and Sophocles, with the concluding evocation of Sophocles, "who saw life steadily and saw it whole," standing unencumbered by any additional commentary. His fiction is lucid: while Arnold cannot write poetry to alleviate his "bad days," he can at least write lists of the "clearest-souled of men" to act as mirrors of his own philosophic lack. By thus emphasizing its own emptiness, his poetry produces a literary system in which writers and texts have been substituted for philosophic belief.

The typical Arnoldian crisis poem obsessively rehearses this emptiness by representing a lost and self-conscious reader who can only write about his own condition in reference to Glanvil's Scholar Gipsy, Obermann's icy despair, Wordsworth's nature, Empedocles' suicide, or the pageant of Byron's bleeding heart. Arnold's use of such touchstones is usually taken as proof of his essentially critical turn of mind: Robert Stange suggests that there is "no other poetry in English which explores a literary theory in such fullness and depth." This theory, however, is never simply scholarly, for it allows Arnold to manipulate a philosophic aura through his reference to writers with whom he can claim intimacy. His familiarity with Wordsworth, for example, grants him access to the rhetoric of nature, allowing him to exercise a certain control over that language, because he chooses to speak with such reverential authority about Wordsworth himself. The forbidding conceptual realm of formulating a philosophic system is thus humanized by Arnold's role as a quaintly Victorian reader of past systems, and the loss of belief that the poems mourn becomes a background against which Arnold can move freely and efficiently between beliefs. This movement constitutes Arnold's form of philosophical organization: he translates the necessity of belief into specific literary figures and texts; in addressing and ordering them he implicitly creates his own philosophic framework, or another method to contain anarchy within culture.

Much as Arnold converts writers who are important to him into single-minded figures of belief, he increasingly justified his poetry because it was emblematic of the key philosophic dilemma of his age. As he wrote to his sister, "My poems represent, on the whole, the main movement of mind of the last quarter of a century, and thus they will probably have their day as people become conscious of what that movement of mind is." The poems are authentic because they are literal transcriptions of the times, because they chart the movement of wandering between two worlds, with all the excessive nostalgia and melancholy associated with it. That Arnold judiciously chose a poetry of loss because it was in consonance with the philosophic mood of his time presents his melancholy as a deliberated and chosen echo of belief, suggesting a design in which it is only fitting that a post-Romantic poet should express depletion and philosophic failure, in order that he remain believable.

The idea of loss in Arnold's poetry is therefore a convenience in which he assembles catchphrases of other times and writers, such as nature, joy, alienation, faith, and skepticism, and juggles them with a faithless dexterity. Arnold cajoles and desires the disappearance of faith that leaves him without any coherent framework, causing him to wander in what J. Hillis Miller describes as "a space without coordinates, center, or goal . . . to be in one place in this uncharted space is the same as to be in any other place, for there are no paths or signposts by which the hapless wanderer might tell what origin he has left or what end he might seek." Miller takes the unanchored despair that characterizes poems like "Stanzas from the Grande Chartreuse" and "The Scholar-Gipsy" at face value, choosing to minimize their crucial technique of using literature and the mythic figures that can be extracted from it as signposts and as a method of ordering Arnold's historical moment. The very act of contrasting the presence of faith in a previous era with the lack of one in the Arnoldian present becomes a reverse surrogate for a statement of belief and commitment, just as Arnold's habit of drawing attention to the fact that he is not a Goethe or a Wordsworth indirectly taps a rhetoric that the poet continually and excessively professes to lack. The "uncharted space" of his melancholy is thus given an anchor and a distinct sense of historical know-how through the authority with which Arnold populates his poems with previous poets, making his language of loss far more efficient than it first appears to be. That he manipulates rather than merely expresses loss is compounded by the fact that the critic's admiration of his touchstones appears to be so hugely uncritical. While poems like "Memorial Verses" and "The Youth of Nature" may celebrate Wordsworth's "healing power" and his ability to "make us feel," they make Wordsworth one with a simplistic reading of nature that, by implication, Arnold is too fallen and educated to share. Rather than being an amorphous expression of defeat, Arnold's despair comes equipped with the sharp edge of an intelligent choice, compensating for an absence of belief by summoning up previous modes of believing, and taking a reader's revenge in the judgments it passes on them.

That Arnold's revenge most often takes the form of a studied praise of his precursors indicates the dexterity with which he calls attention to his own secondariness. He is always in waiting for what Harold Bloom calls the "anxiety in expectation of being flooded," but by converting belatedness into his brand of pleasing melancholy, Arnold is empowered by defeat. This complicated strategy runs through most of his poems of loss, but is most clearly literalized in the dialectic on which I wish to focus, which is Arnold's long battle with his own text, *Empedocles on Etna*. The poem that Arnold edited out of his own canon, only reprinted in 1868 "at the request of a man of genius . . . Mr. Robert Browning," illustrates the breaking point of his idea of integrity where neither the use of distant, safely literary examples nor the reverence of a reader can unite the disparities that are Matthew Arnold into a cultural mobile. *Empedocles on Etna* is a crucially important text on two levels: the poem's disaffection with philosophic readings is an embarrassment in Arnold's cultural project, and the consequent self-revenge of his reading of *Empedocles on Etna* in the 1853 Preface to the *Poems* demonstrates his ability to worm a way into safety by presenting himself as a weak touchstone for a problem that must be observed, avoided, and excised from the canon. The text is seditious because, instead of conserving the fine integrity of the Hellenic ideal, it reads Arnold's version of modernity into Hellenism, thereby admitting relativity into the fundamental example of sweetness and light. In the celebrated formula of the Preface:

> Into the feelings of a man so situated there entered much that we
> are accustomed to consider as exclusively modern . . . the calm,
> the cheerfulness, the disinterested objectivity have disappeared;
> the dialogue of the mind with itself has commenced; we already
> hear the doubts, we witness the discouragement, of Hamlet and
> of Faust.

The jittery aggression of this act of banishment is concealed by the "disinterested objectivity" with which Arnold scrutinises his own poems, which again seeks to establish the transcendence of a figurative and intelligent reader over the text. Yet however much the Preface attempts to hide Arnold's inability to keep his system intact, the poem itself is a sharp reminder of the fallibility and entrepreneurship of his reading of culture.

In *Culture and Anarchy*, Arnold defends his "unsystematic" definition of culture with a disclaimer: "From a man without a philosophy no one can expect philosophical completeness . . . clearness is the one merit which a plain, unsystematic writer, without a philosophy, can hope to have." This "clearness" is no doubt in operation when Arnold describes and lists the miraculous powers of culture: "Culture looks beyond machinery, culture hates hatred; culture has one great passion, the passion for sweetness and light. It has one even yet greater!—the passion for making them *prevail*." Culture, then, like his Victorian version of romanticism, is a construct that feels, sees, possesses passion; it is equally solicitous of the secret spaces of morality: Culture "places human perfection in an internal condition, in the growth and predominance of our humanity proper. . . . Not a having and a resting, but a growing and a becoming, is the character of perfection as culture conceives it." The overabundance that Arnold ascribes to Culture is again in keeping with a romantic plenitude that Arnold always claims to lack, the crucial wrinkle being that Arnold's cultural "growing and becoming" is deeply fearful of historical process, in that "real" change, with its concomitant loss of faith, and its disintegration into iron times, is an antagonist that culture has to reckon with and defeat. While the recurring problematic in Arnold's reading of his precursors is the attempt to demonstrate the compatibility between revolution and nature, his substitute concept, culture, has anarchy as its clearly demarcated enemy: it works in the face of change to uphold the memorializing and secretly effete ideals of literary Hellenism—sweetness and light—and the hierarchy of touchstones.

On the surface, *Empedocles on Etna* appears to project such an authority of culture: Empedocles as hero is easily interpreted as a belated but heroic emblem of culture, besieged by a world of sophistry and change. And so, he can be read as a more resourceful version of Arnold, who Alan Roper claims is "sufficiently Arnoldian to have learned to doubt his metaphysic, but sufficiently unArnoldian to be capable of a final assertion that his metaphysic still has validity." The problem is, however, that this metaphysic leads to extinction: unlike "Obermann," whose icy despair leaves the narrator a sadder and a wiser man but one who at least has the advantage of still being alive and reading, Empedocles' end is alleviated only by the immature lyricism of a belated audience, as epitomized by Callicles. As a consequence, cultural mobility rather than historical change is under attack: unlike the typical Arnoldian crisis poem, *Empedocles* is the one poem in which change is not counterbalanced and contained by the fine, literary coda, and the text consists of a mapping out of the disintegration of the coda itself.

In a more obvious manifestation of Arnold's disaffection, however, the redeeming presence of a reader who can recollect and thus conserve the artifacts of culture is replaced by a tired reader, Empedocles, who believes that "I read in all things my own deadness." The cultural past does not resuscitate Empedocles, which makes him a subversive enemy in Arnold's narcissistic universe. To Empedocles, the cultural project is not only an insufficient rhetorical framework but is also a redundance, illustrating only the methodological futility with which "we search out dead men's words, and works of dead men's hands." In tracing Empedocles' alienation from his world, Arnold comes precariously close to repudiating the viability of cultural mobility and its efficacy to act as a philosophic system that an attentive reader can locate and then assess. For the dreariness of *Empedocles* tests the good faith of the most attentive reader to a breaking point.

The structure of the poem rests on the failure of dialogue between the protagonist and his two readers, Pausanias and Callicles, which anticipates an equivalent failure between poem and audience. Pausanias begs of the master the healing of fiction, the secret of Pantheia's miraculous cure that can serve to resuscitate his vision of Empedocles as a vital center of authority and knowledge. What he receives is a solemn song that can be seen as a direct statement of the narrative's philosophical stoicism, but which is equally an attack on the possibility of reading: although Empedocles begins with an injunction to turn inward and seek a buried life—"Once read thy own breast right, / And thou hast done with fears"—he proceeds to deny the validity of any "right" reading. As in Arnold's lyric, "The Buried Life," desire is synonymous with impossibility, and rather than incompletion leading to a Wordsworthian endorsement of "something ever more about to be," it produces only an idiom of entropy and waste. For if the privacy of the mind cannot be read, then Empedocles also denies any coherence to the paraphernalia of culture:

> We scrutinise the dates
> Of long-past human things,
> The bounds of effaced states,
> The lines of deceased kings;
> We search out dead men's words, and works of dead men's
>   hands;
>
> . . . .
>
> But still, as we proceed
> The mass swells more and more
> Of volumes yet to read,
> Of secrets yet to explore.

In his function as the figure of a writer, or a potential source of a philosophic system, Empedocles as poet denies his audience access to any touchstone that could serve as a replication of his former philosophy. The poem thus nudges Arnold's fundamental method in the ribs, for rather than providing a belated reader with the possibility of a plangent discourse, Empedocles as a Victorian writer seeks to withdraw his name from circulation and to adopt instead the precariously inverted posture of a failed reader. Unlike the structure of Arnold's "literary" lyrics, in which the poet as agonized reader seeks to engage mythic figures of power in a historic dialogue for literary control, *Empedocles on Etna* entertains the dangers of modernity by allowing the two emblems of writer and reader to coalesce into the same monotone. Culture gains the victory when Arnold as narrator props his mind in these bad days by balancing his impotent intelligence with the potent joys of a Wordsworth, Goethe, Byron: culture caves in on itself when Empedocles berates his failure to be his own image of strength by the "charred, blackened, melancholy waste" of "Etna's great mouth." In the geography of Arnold's poem, the receptacle that is Etna is a hole, a disposal system that consumes rather than conserves the artifacts of culture: when Empedocles cries "Receive me, hide me, quench me, take me home!" he addresses an indifferent and ahistorical structure that is far less accommodating than the poignantly outdated architecture of the Grande Chartreuse. There, the narrator of the poem (and the reader of its iron times) is at least situated in a historical confluence, and it is out of the conflict of opposing systems that he can plead: "Oh, hide me in your gloom profound, / Ye solemn seats of holy pain! / Take me, cowled forms, and fence me round, / Till I possess my soul again." Even where Arnold, in the consistently relinquished idiom of his lyric crises, knows he is only pleading with a relic, his voice is still housed by the notion of continuity and the fiction of being a lesser shadow of a stronger past. In the flat narrative of Empedocles, however, relic (the past writer) and remainder (the present reader) are represented as oddly identical.

In act 1 of this singularly undramatic poem, Empedocles is able to dispense with the idea of culture through his denial of his audience, Pausanias: his stoical injunction towards "moderate bliss" and moderate desire are indications of his repudiation of his status as a cultural symbol for desire. Rather than resignation, he expresses acquiescence to the notion of redundancy by recognizing indifference within his own writerly desire. His stoicism is as a consequence savagely ironic, for it is founded upon principles of destitution in its vision of a "patiently exact" deity, whose functions are mechanistic and industrial:

> And patiently exact
> This universal God
> Alike to any act
> Proceeds at any nod
> And quietly declaims the cursings of himself.

Empedocles robs culture of its magic by refusing to participate in mythic structures, such as the miracle of Pantheia, or the reverberations of Etna, that Callicles' songs invoke ("These rumblings are not Typho's groans, I know!"). As a philosopher / magician, he stands as a mediator between the cultural presence of Pausanias the questioner and the natural presence of Callicles the potential poet, but he absents himself from the task of fulfilling the need of either. Thus when in act 2 Empedocles repudiates the role of the magician, Arnold offers a revision of Prospero's disrobing that neither liberates magic into a natural habitat nor leaves the magician reconciled to return to culture as a dying man. Instead, Empedocles' rejection of his charms reveals only his disaffection with the "fool's armoury of magic," and its potential as a symbolic acceptance of death is reduced to a mere gesture of fatigue.

As an emblem of reading, Empedocles' suicide is already accomplished before the action of the poem, since he remains a deadweight on the narrative, and barely swerves from his sullen knowledge of belittlement: "I alone / Am dead to life and joy, therefore I read / In all things my own deadness." His inability to respond in any lasting way to Callicles' lyricism creates a curious, disjunction in the text, as Callicles' songs become progressively more peripheral to the course of Empedocles' monologues. Through them, evocations of a Wordsworthian nature become diffused, and are reduced to charming literary moments that can function only as anachronisms. The harp-player's lyrics are consequently more double-edged than they first appear, for instead of providing a counterpoint to the philosopher's despair, they corroborate the deadness of the poetic situation by remaining autonomous and indifferent points of punctuation that can in no way ameliorate the central claustrophobia of the poem. Callicles is thus a synecdoche for the failure of dialogue, or the inefficacy of reading upon which *Empedocles on Etna* is based. The survivors in Arnold's narrative poems often serve a double-edged function: Callicles is an example of both an aesthetic and a post-romantic continuity, in that he at least keeps on singing, and also an illustration of the benign irrelevance of such an aestheticism.

To survive as reader requires a certain obstinacy, and as such Callicles out-reads Empedocles by insisting on repeating the pure form of lyric narcissism that will not take too much cognisance of the crises that history engenders. Callicles as the poet of innocence thus both survives the burden of the poem and indirectly embodies the untrustworthy texture of Arnold's commitment to integrity. Here, he resembles Iseult of Brittany in "Tristram and Iseult": the surviving, meeker Iseult is usually seen as Arnold's means of softening the violent fable of passionate attachment and identifying with the dregs of mythic history. Once the writers and prime actors of the myth, Tristram and Iseult of Cornwall, have vacated the poem, the second Iseult, Arnold suggests, remains to perpetuate the more Victorian virtues of endurance and motherhood. Arnold as reader tries to hide his anxiety about the second Iseult's version of romance: she indeed survives in softer key, but however unsuitably, she assumes the role of the storyteller who knows how to outlast her larger competitors.

Much as Arnold wishes to be modest about his equation with the grandiosity of romance, the second Iseult acts as a reader of the Romantic past who subverts rather than enhances the possibility of the liaison Arnold desired to construct, between mythology and history. The tale Iseult chooses to tell her children illustrates the impotence of the magician: Merlin is seduced by Vivian, left disrobed and unarmed, but rather than confirming the violence of love that could provide some validity to Iseult's remaining life, her story centers on love's frivolity. Merlin is "left prisoner till the judgment-day" while Vivian the enchantress is left free to wander, not because of any fierce rejection of the magician, but for the peripheral, vagrant reason that concludes the poem: "For she was passing weary of his love." Iseult's final tale renders passion obsolete, for it deftly moves beyond being a mere chronicle of the tragedy of romantic action to illustrate, much as Arnold's Wordsworthian poems do, the curious redundance of a commitment to feeling.

In a similarly self-belittling vengeance, Callicles' lyrics fail to provide a "natural" counterpoint to Empedocles' dark intellectual despair: instead, by reviving a deliberately limited genre, they recuperate the text only through a perfunctory lip-service. While the charm of the final lyric of *Empedocles* is often read as Arnold's failure to reconcile his impulse towards elegance with the more tragic demands of the poem's elegaic conclusion, the very academic nature of such lyrical gestures constitutes the poem's most startling reversal. Empedocles' suicide represents the consumption of philosophy by historical process, through which the "sophist-brood" overlays "the last spark of man's consciousness with words." What remains is only the peripheral language of lyricism, or a voice that is fully conscious of the quaintness of its idiom. In act 1, Callicles already knows that he must dismiss the idea of miracle as superstition and also knows that Empedocles needs to be distracted from his need for authority: "Keep his mind from preying on itself, / And talk to him of things at hand and common." By the end of the poem, Callicles has become a detached method of distraction: much like Iseult of Brittany, he gives the sharp edge of modernity to the structure of nostalgic tale-telling.

Callicles' final lyric song thus constitutes the emptying of Arnoldian reading. He is the potential poet who studiously avoids addressing the vocabulary of philosophical self-consumption that is Empedocles' end, and instead offers a winsome account of how the gods and muses must vacate the terrain that the pubescent poet now inhabits. Etna, like the productions of romanticism, "heaves fiercely" over the harp-player, but he can adroitly avoid being overpowered by informing the sources of his inspiration that they must retire: "Not here, O Apollo! / Are haunts meet for thee." The neutrality of this pronouncement indicates the exquisite energy of *Empedocles on Etna:* the poem is careless about outdated philosophers and their tragic ends, but equally and charmingly careless about latter-day poets who know they are slender and only incidentally pretty.

Through the figure of Callicles, *Empedocles on Etna* subverts not only a sense of dialogue between a tragic actor and his audience, but also suggests that the dialogue of the mind with itself has been outmoded. In place of a culture that is essentially a growing and becoming, the poem offers its solace through a perversely wistful reconstitution of the idea of a cultural past. The final song of the poem—a competent rewriting of Hesiod—is not really concerned with illustrating the "calm, the cheerfulness, the disinterested

objectivity" of Hellenism, and instead is content to offer culture as an academic proposition: as Iseult of Brittany is incapable of heroic love but can
acutely illustrate the exhaustion of passion through her tale, Callicles as the
survivor of Arnold's poem suggests the virtue of neutrality. He does not aim
to belong to the haunts meet for Apollo, and his Victorian replay of Hellenism
justly illustrates the absence of the muses, but does not prevent him from
listing and naming the subjects suitable to their hymns:

> The day in his hotness,
> The strife with the palm;
> The night in her silence,
> The stars in their calm.

The business of tragic encounter is vitiated by his idiom, but rather than
illustrating Arnold's failure to deal with tragedy, it points instead to the
cunning power of the historically peripheral. If Wordsworth is too natural
to be true, the Scholar Gypsy too shy to be spied, and Empedocles too dead
to be alive, there still remains Arnold as reader of them all, sustained by his
ability to be so strategically minor.

To censor *Empedocles on Etna* as Arnold did, because it attacks the great
system of culture, or as later critics have done, because it fails to revive a
tragic vision and thus "ironically mocks the Olympian prescriptions that
Arnold handed down in the Preface," is to ignore the hidden strategy of
readership that gives the text its power to survive in the Victorian canon.
Arnold cannot claim to have substituted a Victorian rhetoric of culture in
place of a Romantic rhetoric of nature thus engendering the development of
a new but equally passionate system: on this ground, *Empedocles* in particular
contradicts Arnold's ostensible purpose, and calls for the censorship of the
judicious critic. But as a complicated expression of Arnold's fiction of being
"only a reader," *Empedocles on Etna* is energy efficient because it converts the
anxiety of belatedness into a period piece. As a remaining poet, Callicles'
slight lyrics glance off and away from the huge rhetoric of a tired Empedocles:
like Arnold, he can daintily ask: "For what avail'd it, all the noise / And
outcry of the former men?" An Arnoldian reader gathers strength through
replicating this noise in the minor key of pleasing melancholy, by returning
to failed systems of belief and charmingly rehearsing their failure. By implication, the Victorian reader constructs history through lamenting its disappearance: Arnold as reader wears his weakness on his sleeve, and, through
carefully reconstructing historic placement as an academic issue, suggests
that in his academics is our peace.

Chronology

1822   Matthew Arnold born December 24, the eldest son of Mary Penrose Arnold and Thomas Arnold, schoolmaster at Laleham-on-Thames. Matthew's godfather is John Keble, a future leader of the Oxford Movement.

1828   Thomas Arnold appointed headmaster of Rugby School.

1831   At Fox How, their vacation home in Westmorland, the Arnolds become friendly with the Wordsworths and with the Claude family, whose daughter Mary was the inspiration for "Marguerite." The Claudes were connected with the international cultural community of French Protestant exiles with ties in Germany and Switzerland.

1836   Matthew Arnold attends Winchester, his father's old school; begins writing verse; tours France with his parents during the summer.

1837–40   Attends Rugby School, where he becomes friends with Arthur Hugh Clough, Thomas Hughes, and Arthur Penrhyn, later Thomas Arnold's biographer; receives various literary awards; wins an open scholarship to Balliol College, Oxford.

1841   Enters Balliol College, Oxford. Balliol is the center of the Oxford Movement, which his father vehemently opposes. Arnold shows little interest in the movement. He passes time punting on the Cherwell and wandering through the Cumnor Hills with Clough and A. P. Stanley. He reads Carlyle, Emerson, and George Sand, and later Goethe and Spinoza.

1842   Thomas Arnold dies suddenly of heart failure.

1843 – 44   Arnold wins the Newdigate Poetry Prize with *Cromwell*. He graduates with only second-class honors, owing to his neglect of his studies.

1845 – 48   After serving for a short time as assistant-master at Rugby, Arnold becomes private secretary to the Marquis of Lansdowne. While on one of several trips to the Continent, he admires the French actress Rachel, subject of three later sonnets. During this time, he probably begins reading Senancour and Sainte-Beuve. On a holiday walking tour in Switzerland, he is disappointed when the "Marguerite" of his poems, Mary Claude, fails to meet him in Thun, thus ending his hopes for further development of a long-standing romantic attachment.

1849   *The Strayed Reveller, and Other Poems.*

1850   "Memorial Verses" published, following the death of Wordsworth. Arnold begins to court Frances Lucy Wightman, the daughter of Sir William Wightman, Justice of the Queen's Bench. Because of his low income, he is unwelcome as a suitor.

1851   Arnold appointed Inspector of Schools, a job which will require him to spend much of the next thirty-five years traveling throughout England and Wales. He marries Frances Lucy Wightman, "Flu." On their honeymoon, he visits the Grande Chartreuse. They settle in London.

1852   *Empedocles on Etna, and Other Poems.*

1853   *Poems*, a selection from earlier volumes with several new poems, including "The Scholar-Gipsy" and "Sohrab and Rustum." The Preface explains the omission of *Empedocles*, condemning it as a sterile, modern "dialogue of the mind with itself."

1855   *Poems, Second Series*, a further selection from past volumes plus a few new poems, including "Balder Dead." "Stanzas from the Grande Chartreuse" and "Haworth Churchyard."

1857   Arnold elected Professor of Poetry at Oxford. His inaugural lecture, "On the Modern Element in Literature," is the first to be delivered in English rather than Latin.

1858   *Merope.*

1859–61   Travels extensively in Europe on a commission to investigate popular education; meets Sainte-Beuve and other leading intellectuals; publishes several studies on educational and political matters, including *England and the Italian Question* and *The Popular Education of France*. His Oxford Lectures, *On Translating Homer*, are also published. Longtime friend Clough dies.

1865   *Essays in Criticism*.

1866   "Thyrsis," elegy for Clough.

1867   *New Poems* (includes the first reprinting of *Empedocles on Etna*, and *On the Study of Celtic Literature* (Oxford lectures).

1868   Basil, Matthew Arnold's infant son, dies in January. In November, his eldest son, Thomas, dies at the age of sixteen.

1869   *Culture and Anarchy*, "Obermann," and "Sainte-Beuve."

1870   *St. Paul and Protestantism*.

1871   *Friendship's Garland*, a series of humorous letters on English life and culture originally printed in the *Pall Mall Gazette*.

1872   William Trevenen Arnold, Matthew Arnold's son, dies at age eighteen.

1873   *Literature and Dogma*, Arnold's most important work on religion.

1875   Objections to *Literature and Dogma* answered in *God and the Bible*.

1876   George Sand dies.

1877   *Last Essays on Church and Religion* and a commemorative essay on George Sand.

1879   *Mixed Essays* and selected *Poems of Wordsworth*.

1881   Selected *Poetry of Byron*.

1882   "Westminster Abbey," the elegy for A. P. Stanley, the late Dean of Westminster; *Irish Essays and Others*.

1883–86   Lecture tour of the United States. The lectures are published as *Discourses in America*. He returns to the United States to visit his daughter, married to an American. Retires from Inspectorship of Schools.

1888   Arnold dies suddenly of heart failure while waiting in Liv-
        erpool for the arrival of his daughter from America. *Essays in
        Criticism, Second Series* published posthumously.

Contributors

HAROLD BLOOM, Sterling Professor of the Humanities at Yale University, is the author of *The Anxiety of Influence*, *Poetry and Repression*, and many other volumes of literary criticism. His forthcoming study, *Freud: Transference and Authority*, attempts a full-scale reading of all of Freud's major writings. A MacArthur Prize Fellow, he is the general editor of five series of literary criticism published by Chelsea House.

W. H. AUDEN, prolific playwright and literary critic as well as one of the most acclaimed poets of this century, is himself the subject of a volume in the Chelsea House series Modern Critical Views. Among his critical works are *The Enchafèd Flood*, *Making, Knowing and Judging*, and *Secondary Worlds*.

J. HILLIS MILLER is Gray Professor of Rhetoric at Yale University. He is the best-known spokesman for the Geneva school of criticism of Georges Poulet and for the deconstructive criticism of Jacques Derrida and the late Paul de Man. His books include *The Form of Victorian Fiction*, *The Disappearance of God*, *Poets of Reality*, *Thomas Hardy: Distance and Desire*, and *Fiction and Repetition*.

GEOFFREY TILLOTSON is Professor of English Literature at Birkbeck College, University of London. He is the author of *Augustan Studies*, *A View of Victorian Literature*, *Thackeray the Novelist*, and *Mid-Victorian Studies* with Kathleen Tillotson.

G. WILSON KNIGHT was one of the foremost literary critics of our time. In addition to his well-known books on Shakespeare, *The Wheel of Fire*, *The Imperial Theme*, and others, he wrote highly regarded studies of Romanticism and poetic tradition, including *The Starlit Dome*, *The Burning Oracle*, and *The Christian Renaissance*.

WILLIAM ROBBINS, formerly Professor of English at the University of

British Columbia, is a Fellow of the Royal Society of Canada. His books include *The Ethical Idealism of Matthew Arnold*, *The Newman Brothers*, and *Humanistic Values in English Literature*.

WILLIAM E. BUCKLER is Professor of English at New York University. He is the author of *Prose of the Victorian Period*, *The Major Victorian Poets*, and *The Victorian Imagination: Essays in Aesthetic Exploration*.

RUTH apROBERTS is Professor of English at the University of California, Berkeley. A former Guggenheim Fellow, she is the author of *The Moral Trollope* and several studies of poetry and religion.

A. DWIGHT CULLER is Emily Sanford Professor of English at Yale University. His critical works include *The Imperial Intellect: A Study of Newman's Educational Ideal*, *The Poetry of Tennyson*, *The Victorian Mirror of History*, and many important essays on Matthew Arnold and Victorian literature.

SARA SULERI is Assistant Professor of English at Yale University and coeditor of *The Yale Journal of Criticism*. Her book in progress is on Wordsworth, Arnold, and Yeats.

Bibliography

Alexander, Edward. *Matthew Arnold and John Stuart Mill*. New York: Columbia University Press, 1968.

———. *Matthew Arnold, John Ruskin, and the Modern Temper*. Columbus: Ohio State University Press, 1973.

Allott, Kenneth A. "A Background for *Empedocles on Etna*. In *Essays and Studies 1968*, edited by Simeon Potter. London: John Murray, 1968.

———. *Matthew Arnold*. London: Longmans, Green, 1962.

———. "Matthew Arnold's Reading-Lists in Three Early Diaries." *Victorian Studies* 2 (1959): 254–66.

Allott, Miriam. "Arnold and 'Marguerite—Continued'." *Victorian Poetry* 23 (1985): 125–44.

———. "Matthew Arnold: 'All One and Continuous.' " In *The Victorian Experience: The Poets*, edited by Richard A. Levine, 67–93. Athens: Ohio University Press, 1982.

Anderson, Warren D. *Matthew Arnold and the Classical Tradition*. Ann Arbor: University of Michigan Press, 1965.

Armstrong, Isobel, comp. *Victorian Scrutinies: Reviews of Poetry 1830–1870*. London: Athlone, 1972.

Baldick, Chris. "Matthew Arnold's Innocent Language." In *The Social Mission of English Criticism 1848–1930*. Oxford: Oxford University Press, 1983.

Bate, Walter Jackson. "Matthew Arnold." In *Criticism: The Major Texts*, 437–43. New York: Harcourt, Brace & World, 1952.

Baum, Paul F., ed. *Ten Studies in the Poetry of Matthew Arnold*. Durham, N.C.: Duke University Press, 1958.

Berlin, James A. "Arnold's Two Poets: The Critical Context." *Studies in English Literature 1500–1900* 23 (1983): 615–31.

Bourke, John. "The Notion of Isolation in Matthew Arnold." *Notes and Queries* 198 (1953): 166–67.

Brown, E. K. "Matthew Arnold and the Eighteenth Century." *University of Toronto Quarterly* 9 (1940): 202–13.

———. *Matthew Arnold: A Study in Conflict*. Chicago: University of Chicago Press, 1944.

Buckley, Vincent. *Poetry and Morality: Studies on the Criticism of Matthew Arnold, T. S. Eliot, and F. R. Leavis*. London: Chatto & Windus, 1959.

Bush, Douglas. *Matthew Arnold: A Survey of His Poetry and Prose*. New York: Macmillan, 1971.

Carroll, Joseph. *The Cultural Theory of Matthew Arnold*. Berkeley: University of California Press, 1982.

Chambers, E. K. *Matthew Arnold: A Study*. Oxford: Oxford University Press, Clarendon Press, 1947.

Coulling, Sidney M. B. *Matthew Arnold and His Critics: A Study of His Controversies*. Athens: Ohio University Press, 1974.

————. "Matthew Arnold's 1853 Preface: Its Origin and Aftermath." *Victorian Studies* 7 (1964): 233–63.

Culler, A. Dwight. "Arnold and Etna." In *Victorian Essays: A Symposium*, edited by Warren D. Anderson and Thomas D. Clareson, 44–59. Kent, Ohio: Kent State University Press, 1967.

————. *Imaginative Reason: The Poetry of Matthew Arnold*. New Haven: Yale University Press, 1966.

————. "No Arnold Could Ever Write a Novel." *Victorian Newsletter* 29 (1966): 1–5.

Curgenven, J. P. " 'The Scholar-Gipsy': A Study of the Growth, Meaning, and Integration of a Poem." *Litera* (Turkey) 2 (1955).

Dale, Peter. *The Victorian Critic and the Idea of History: Carlyle, Arnold, and Pater*. Cambridge: Harvard University Press, 1977.

Davis, Arthur Kyle, Jr. *Matthew Arnold's Letters: A Descriptive Checklist*. Charlottesville: University of Virginia Press, 1968.

Dawson, Carl, ed. *Matthew Arnold: The Poetry*. London: Routledge & Kegan Paul, 1973.

DeLaura, David J. "Arnold and Carlyle." *PMLA* 79 (1964): 104–29.

————. *Hebrew and Hellene in Victorian England: Newman, Arnold, and Pater*. Austin: University of Texas Press, 1969.

————. "Matthew Arnold's Religious and Historical Vision." *Dissertation Abstracts* 21 (1961): 3085.

————., ed. *Matthew Arnold: A Collection of Critical Essays*. Englewood Cliffs, N.J.: Prentice-Hall, 1973.

Donovan, Robert A. "The Method of Arnold's *Essays in Criticism*." *PMLA* 71 (1956): 922–31.

Dudley, Fred A. "Matthew Arnold and Science." *PMLA* 57 (1942): 275–94.

Duffin, Henry Charles. *Arnold the Poet*. London: Bowes & Bowes, 1962.

Ebel, Henry. "Matthew Arnold and Classical Culture." *Arion* 2 (1965): 188–220.

Eells, John Shepard, Jr. *The Touchstones of Matthew Arnold*. New York: Bookman Associates, 1955.

Eggenswiller, David L. "Arnold's Passive Questers." *Victorian Poetry* 5 (1967): 1–11.

Eliot, T. S. "Arnold and Pater." In *Selected Essays 1917–1932*. London: Faber & Faber, 1932.

————. "Matthew Arnold." In *The Use of Poetry and the Use of Criticism*, 95–112. Cambridge: Harvard University Press, 1933.

Farrell, John P. "Matthew Arnold's Tragic Vision." *PMLA* 85 (1970): 107–17.

Faverty, Frederick E. *Matthew Arnold the Ethnologist*. Evanston, Ill.: Northwestern University Press, 1951.

Fletcher, Pauline. "Arnold: The Forest Glade." In *Gardens and Grim Ravines: The Language of Landscape in Victorian Poetry*, 72–100. Princeton: Princeton University Press, 1983.

Forster, E. M. "Text and Context: E. M. Forster on Matthew Arnold." BBC Broadcast, November 16, 1964.

Forsyth, R. A. " 'The Buried Life'—The Contrasting Views of Arnold and Clough in the Context of Dr. Arnold's Historiography." *ELH* 35 (1968): 218–53.

Goodheart, Eugene, George Levine, Morris Dickstein, and Stuart Tave. "The Function of Matthew Arnold at the Present Time." *Critical Inquiry* 9 (1983): 451–515.

Gottfried, Leon. *Matthew Arnold and the Romantics*. London: Routledge & Kegan Paul, 1963.

Hecht, Anthony. "The Dover Bitch (A Criticism of Life)." *Transatlantic Review* 2 (1960): 57–58.

Honan, Park. "The Character of Marguerite in Arnold's *Switzerland*." *Victorian Poetry* 23 (1985).

———. *Matthew Arnold: A Life*. New York: McGraw-Hill, 1981.

Houghton, Walter E. "Arnold's *Empedocles on Etna*." *Victorian Studies* 1 (1958): 311–36.

James, D. G. *Matthew Arnold and the Decline of English Romanticism*. Oxford: Oxford University Press, Clarendon Press, 1961.

Johnson, E. D. H. *The Alien Vision of Victorian Poetry*. 1952. Reprint. Hamden, Conn.: Archon, 1963: 147–213.

Johnson, Stacy W. *The Voices of Matthew Arnold*. New Haven: Yale University Press, 1961.

Kelleher, John V. "Matthew Arnold and the Celtic Revival." In *Perspectives of Criticism*, edited by Harry Levin, 197–221. Cambridge: Harvard University Press, 1950.

Kermode, Frank. *The Romantic Image*. 1957. Reprint. New York: Vintage, 1964.

Kreiger, Murray. "The Critical Legacy of Matthew Arnold: Or, The Strange Brotherhood of T. S. Eliot, I. A. Richards, and Northrop Frye." *The Southern Review* 5 (1969): 457–74.

———. " 'Dover Beach' and the Tragic Sense of Eternal Recurrence." *University of Kansas City Review* 23 (1956): 73–79.

Lewis, Wyndham. "Matthew Arnold." *Times Literary Supplement* (August 6, 1954).

Lucas, F. L. "Matthew Arnold." In *Victorian Literature: Modern Essays in Criticism*, edited by Austin Wright. New York: Oxford University Press, 1961.

McCarthy, Patrick J. *Matthew Arnold and the Three Classes*. New York: Columbia University Press, 1964.

Madden, William A. *Matthew Arnold: A Study of the Aesthetic Temperament in Victorian England*. Bloomington: Indiana University Press, 1964.

Neiman, Fraser. "The Zeitgeist of Matthew Arnold." *PMLA* 72 (1957): 977–78.

Orrick, James Bentley. *Matthew Arnold and Goethe*. 1928. Reprint. London: William Dawson, 1966.

Pearson, Gabriel. "The Importance of Arnold's *Merope*." In *The Major Victorian Poets*, edited by Isobel Armstrong, 225–52. Lincoln: University of Nebraska Press, 1969.

Ray, Linda Lee. "Callicles on Etna: The Other Mask." *Victorian Poetry* 7 (1969): 309–20.

Robbins, William. *The Ethical Idealism of Matthew Arnold*. Toronto: University of Toronto Press, 1959.

Roper, Alan. *Arnold's Poetic Landscapes*. Baltimore: The Johns Hopkins University Press, 1969.

Rowse, A. L. *Matthew Arnold: Poet and Prophet*. London: Thames & Hudson, 1976.

Runcie, C. A. "Matthew Arnold and Myth: A Reading of the Preface to *Poems, 1853.*" *Journal of the Australian Universities Language and Literature Association* 37 (1972): 5–17.

Sagovsky, Nicholas. *Between Two Worlds: George Tyrell's Relationship to the Thought of Matthew Arnold*. Cambridge: Cambridge University Press, 1983.

Schneider, Mary. "The Arnoldian Voice in Woolf's *The Waves*." *The Arnoldian* 10 (1983): 7–20.

Shurbutt, Sylvia Bailey. "Matthew Arnold's Concept of Nature." *Dissertation Abstracts International* 43 (1982): 1983-A.

Signal, Lillion F. "Matthew Arnold's Search for Wholeness: A Jungian Study." *Dissertation Abstracts International* 44 (1983): 1463-A.

Simpson, James. *Matthew Arnold and Goethe*. London: Modern Humanities Research Association, 1979.

Speller, John L. "Arnold and Immortality." *The Arnoldian* 10 (1983): 21–25.

Stange, G. Robert. *Matthew Arnold: The Poet as Humanist*. Princeton: Princeton University Press, 1967.

Stevenson, Lionel. "Matthew Arnold's Poetry: A Modern Appraisal." *Tennessee Studies in Literature* 4 (1959): 31–41.

Super, R. H. "The Epitome of Matthew Arnold." In *The Victorian Experience: The Prose Writers*, edited by Richard A. Levine. Athens: Ohio University Press, 1982.

———. *The Time-Spirit of Matthew Arnold*. Ann Arbor: University of Michigan Press, 1970.

Taylor, Beverly. "Imagination and Art in Arnold's 'Tristram and Iseult': The Imperative of Making." *Studies in English Literature 1500–1900* 22 (1982): 633–46.

Thorpe, Michael. *Literature in Perspective: Matthew Arnold*. London: Evans Brothers, 1969.

Tinker, C. B., and H. F. Lowry. *The Poetry of Matthew Arnold: A Commentary*. New York: Oxford University Press, 1940.

Trilling, Lionel, "Matthew Arnold." In *Major British Writers*, vol. 2, edited by G. B. Harrison, 579–91. New York: Harcourt, Brace.

———. *Matthew Arnold*. Cleveland: Ohio World Publishing, 1955.

———. "Youth and Arnold," *The Nation* 136 (1933): 211.

Warren, Alba H., Jr. "Matthew Arnold." In *English Poetic Theory: 1825–1865*, 152–70. 1950. Reprint. New York: Octagon Books, 1966.

Wellek, René."Mathew Arnold." In *History of Modern Criticism, 1750–1950: The Later Nineteenth Century*, vol. 4, 155–79. New Haven: Yale University Press, 1965.

Willey, Basil. "Matthew Arnold." In *Nineteenth Century Studies*, 251–83. London: Chatto & Windus, 1949.

Williams, Raymond. "J. H. Newman and Matthew Arnold." In *Culture and Society 1780–1950*, 110–29. 1958. Reprint. New York: Harper & Row, 1966.

Wright, Charles D. "How Matthew Arnold Altered Goethe on Poetry." *Victorian Poetry* 6 (1967): 57–61.

―――. "Matthew Arnold on Heine as 'Continuator of Goethe.' " *Studies in Philology* 65 (1968): 693–701.

Young, Sandra Kay. " 'Things as They Really Are': Disorderly Conduct in Matthew Arnold's Prose." In *Dissertation Abstracts International* 44 (1983): 1452-A.

Zeitlow, Paul, "Heard But Unheeded: The Songs of Callicles in Matthew Arnold's *Empedocles on Etna*." *Victorian Poetry* 21 (1983): 241–56.

Acknowledgments

"Matthew Arnold" by W. H. Auden from *Another Time: Poems* by W. H. Auden, © 1940 and renewed 1968 by W. H. Auden. Reprinted by permission of Random House, Inc. This essay originally appeared in *The English Auden: Essays and Dramtic Writings, 1927–1939*.

"Matthew Arnold" by J. Hillis Miller from *The Disappearance of God: Five Nineteenth-Century Writers* by J. Hillis Miller, © 1963 by the President and Fellows of Harvard College. Reprinted by permission of The Belknap Press of Harvard University Press, Cambridge, Massachusetts.

"Matthew Arnold's Prose: Theory and Practice" by Geoffrey Tillotson from *The Art of Victorian Prose*, edited by George Levine and William Madden, © 1968 by Oxford University Press, Inc. Reprinted by permission of Oxford University Press, Inc.

"The Scholar-Gipsy" by G. Wilson Knight from *Neglected Powers: Essays on Nineteenth and Twentieth Century Literature* by G. Wilson Knight, © 1971 by G. Wilson Knight. Reprinted by permission of Barnes & Noble Books, Totowa, New Jersey and Methuen, Inc.

"Seed-Bed" by William Robbins from *The Arnoldian Principle of Flexibility* (University of Victoria: *English Literary Studies*, 1979), © 1979 by William Robbins. Reprinted by permission of the author and the editor of *English Literary Studies*.

"Arnold and the Crisis of Classicism" by William E. Buckler from *On the Poetry of Matthew Arnold: Essays in Critical Reconstruction* by William E. Buckler, © 1982 by New York University. Reprinted by permission of New York University Press.

"Arnold and God" (originally entitled "Last Essay on Arnold and God") by Ruth apRoberts from *Arnold and God* by Ruth apRoberts, © 1983 by the Regents of the University of California. Reprinted by permission of the University of California Press.

"Matthew Arnold and the Zeitgeist" by A. Dwight Culler from *The Victorian Mirror of History* by A. Dwight Culler, © 1985 by Yale University. Reprinted by permission of the Yale University Press.

"Entropy on Etna: Arnold and the Poetry of Reading" by Sara Suleri, © 1986 by Sara Suleri. Published for the first time in this volume. Printed by permission.

163

Index